The Beautiful Anthology

THE
BEAUTIFUL
ANTHOLOGY

A COLLECTION OF
ESSAYS, STORIES, & POEMS

EDITED BY ELIZABETH COLLINS

 tnb BOOKS

BOOKS

Published by The Nervous Breakdown Books
Los Angeles, California
www.thenervousbreakdown.com

First Edition, June 9, 2012
Copyright © 2012 TNB Books

Book Design: Charlotte Howard, CKH Design
The text is set in Garamond. The titling is set in Rawengulk.

ISBN 098-2-8598-4-8

Printed in the United States of America

CONTENTS

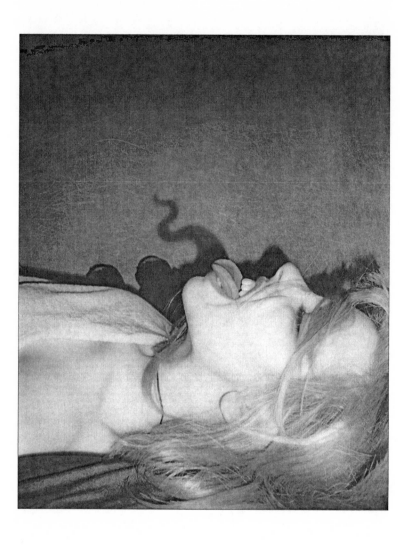

FOREWORD

As I've been reading the many wonderful and refreshingly disparate pieces of writing and art that make up *The Beautiful Anthology*, the French term *belle-laide* keeps coming to mind. Literally translated as "beautiful-ugly," it is an adjective usually given to a woman or girl whose looks are beautiful to some, ugly to others. In short, it denotes a hard-to-pin-down, hard-to-describe woman.

Many people don't understand this term because it seems self-negating, but I think it is a very interesting and appropriate idiom, encapsulating in its way all the dichotomies and debatable areas of life: how one person's beauty, or what one finds beautiful, is not always appreciated by others.

The Beautiful Anthology also captures those gray areas. For example, a tattoo that an adult child gets, defacing a large expanse of her lovely white arm, can ultimately be considered apt and beautiful. The design of urinal dividers can also be a thing of beauty. Seeing the beauty in a perfect tennis serve, in a malodorous, ill-dressed kid covered in dirt, in the parts of our bodies that we usually hate, in death, in all sorts of unexpected places—this is what our anthology is really about.

The very word *anthology* even means—if you don't mind the didactic tendencies of this former English teacher—a collection (or garland) of flowers. Since flowers are the classic example of beauty, *The Beautiful Anthology* is a rather meta title.

The contributors to this anthology are mainly authors who have been featured on the popular literary Web site *The Nervous Breakdown*, founded and directed by *Los Angeles Times* best-selling author Brad Listi. *The Beautiful Anthology* is a publication of TNB Books, the publishing arm of *The Nervous Breakdown*. We have some well-known writers who have kindly shared their work for this project, including Victoria Patterson, Gina Frangello, Jessica Anya Blau, Greg Olear, and Melissa Febos. Likewise, we have many emerging authors (too many to list) and other new and exciting contributors. The artists whose work you will read in this anthology hail from around the world.

You may find some of the work in *Beautiful* to be convention-ally beautiful, and some to be shocking or hard to describe in tradi-tional, sentimental terms. That's exactly the point. This book is, as a whole, *belle-laide*. It should start a conversation about what beauty is and why we find certain things, or people, to be beautiful. It is my hope that *The Beautiful Anthology* will also change readers' minds about beauty and inspire them to share their own stories and to read the work of all of our amazing authors and artists.

— Elizabeth Collins, editor

VICTORIA PATTERSON

THE BEAUTIFUL

WHILE VISITING A RELATIVE AT THE HOSPITAL, I GLANCED OUT the door of her room to the hallway and saw an elderly couple walking. He wore a hospital gown and used a walker. They moved slowly.

As they passed the room, we all made slight gestures of polite acknowledgment – *hello there* – and then they were beyond the open doorway. I was out of their eyesight, though they remained in mine. The man's hospital gown had the featured split in the back. The woman, sensing that I was still watching, moved her hand behind him and closed the gap. Her maneuver was so gentle that it seemed to pass undetected by him. Her hand stayed there, protective, and then they were out of sight.

As a witness, a flash of recognition came over me, and I had a sensation of both the universal and the personal. How many patients have had their gowns protectively covered by loved ones?

And how many not? Hadn't I performed a similar gesture for my grandmother?

Elusive and mysterious combinations of qualities that produce achingly profound sensations fascinate me. This definition of beauty has little to do with physical appearance. It is instinctual, individual, unexpected, and in synch with life (and therefore mystery) itself. I have a respect for, and delight in, beauty at its seemingly most prosaic and incidental.

In *A Portrait of the Artist as a Young Man*, James Joyce describes the mind "arrested and raised above desire and loathing," a comprehension like a flash of sublime recognition. The mind in this mysterious instant the poet Shelley likened to a "fading coal," and the Italian physiologist Luigi Galvani called "the enchantment of the heart." Beauty, Joyce suggests, reveals the illusory divisions between us, and the object of the artist is the creation of the beautiful. To apprehend, to somehow convey and give evidence, is a profound endeavor.

What is beautiful to me defies traditional notions—Leonard Cohen's "crack in everything" that reveals the light. Recently, I did a reading, and the organizer wore a somewhat flamboyant shirt with one side of his collar tucked under. I wanted to reach out my hand and remedy his mistake, but because I didn't know him well enough, I didn't. And no one else did. So his collar remained tucked under, and when I think about that night, what I remember most is his earnestness in beautiful collusion with the collar of his shirt.

A simplistic notion is that beauty is a settled fact, and that what is closest to the standard ideal is closer to beauty. Beauty isn't a material thing, and it doesn't reside in the subject, but in the expression.

What we find beautiful is a reflection of our personality and individuality. It's as beautiful as we think it. We're wrapped up in life, and because we're inundated, because we're human, this is our strongest connection. What is beautiful to me bears a kinship to my life. What moves me is beautiful to me.

When he was in grade school, my eldest son and I came up with a nonverbal form of communication to take the place of those unrestrained preschool and kindergarten hugs and kisses. Before I dropped him off, while still in the car, we'd do a quick "handhold," which, we agreed, meant something akin to "I love you. Have a great day." A last-second affectionate well-wish.

As he got older, the handhold took on different, less obvious variations, until it became a very slight—almost nonexistent—touch of the sides of our pinkies. Now that he's in middle school, I simply imagine it.

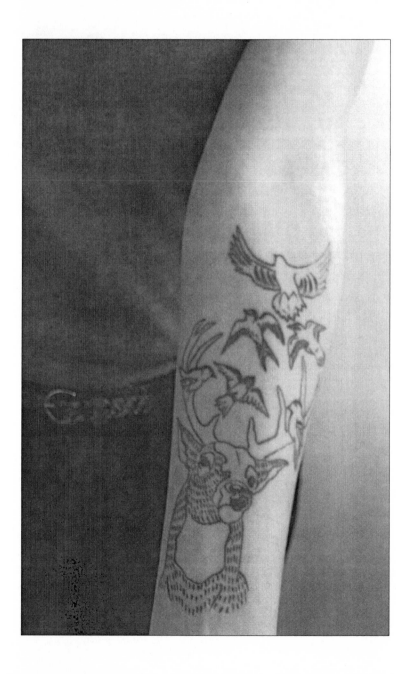

ROBIN ANTALEK

INKED

IGHTEEN YEARS AGO, ON THE WAY TO THE DELIVERY ROOM, the feeling of not being able to stop what was about to happen suddenly overwhelmed me. This baby that had been making me miserable for twenty-four hours had to come out, and the passage of egress was not going to be a gentle one. When my first daughter eventually emerged from her long battle waged in the birth canal, cone-shaped head and bruises on her face the size and shape of peach pits from the last-ditch-effort emergency forceps, a smudge of pink between the delicate fuzz of her brow that one of the nurses deemed an "angel's kiss," I was assured that in a week, maybe less, her face would be healed and the trauma of her birth would leave no visible scars, only memories, where I would be able to chart the ghost marks on her face, badges of what she and I had endured in the moments before her birth.

As the doctors and nurses promised, her face did heal, her complexion, unnaturally tan from a bout of infant jaundice, turned a burnished rose and was smooth to the touch, as if you had dipped your fingers into a pot of cream. Not even a birthmark marred her perfect, brand-new baby flesh. As every new mother does, I inspected her daily from head to toe, kissing the top of her head, her forehead, the tip of her nose, the translucent alabaster insides of her wrists, reassured, at least, from the things I could see on the outside, that she was as normal and beautiful as any baby should be.

As she grew, the only visible mark left over from her birth was the angel's kiss. If she had a high fever or a terrible tantrum, the smudge beneath her bangs would flare a dusty red, like clay, only to disappear when the fever subsided or her demands had been either met or forgotten.

Through toddlerhood to adolescence, my daughter's body endured the regular battle scars of childhood: a cut lip, scraped knees, an irresistible urge to color her face and limbs with markers or paint. When she was four, she had me draw freckles, on a daily basis, across the bridge of her nose with a brown eyeliner pencil—due, in part, to her love of *Pippi Longstocking*. In her early teens, she streaked her hair a rainbow spectrum of pinks, purples, and greens from the little pots of Manic Panic she purchased with baby-sitting money. She rejected the fashion of the mall and, instead, trawled thrift shops and created her own clothing. As a budding artist, she silkscreened T-shirts and drew on everything—bags, notebooks, canvas, paper—until the designs migrated to her jeans, and her hands and her arms were covered with a fine-point black Sharpie.

The hair was just an extension of who she was at the time, and I never balked, instead recalling the advice of a woman with five daughters. Her girls could cut, color, even shave their heads if that's what they desired, she said, as long as they didn't permanently mark or maim their flesh with tattoos or multiple piercings, and I adopted this decree as a casual guideline. "Choose your battles," everyone advised, and so that line in the sand was mine.

I never imagined that I would one day sit next to my firstborn in a tattoo parlor while a stranger bent over her perfect arm with a vibrating needle.

As the person she was soon to be emerged, my daughter's dedication to her art became clearer. She wanted to be a painter. For years, she got up at 6 A.M. every Saturday morning and took a train from our home in Saratoga Springs into New York City to take classes. The colors that had once been on her hair and her body began to surface in her paintings, and by high school graduation, she had been offered a place at each of the top art schools in the country.

So, when my daughter came to her father and me, six months after she had turned eighteen, one month before she would leave for college at the Rhode Island School of Design, and said that she had been thinking about getting a tattoo of her own design, I experienced all over again that moment right before her birth of not being able to stop what was about to happen.

She opened her notebook and slid across the table a piece of paper with a beautifully rendered deer, head and antlers only, and above the antlers, a flock of birds. It was in her classic illustrative style, black on white, the lines clear and steady.

The subject was no surprise. She had been working on a series of paintings of deer over the past year, and these paintings were a huge part of her portfolio. They had been featured in a solo show and in several group shows, and one in particular, two deer against pink wallpaper, had won several major awards. While the animals were always realistic, each of the paintings was a stark contrast of juxta-position, with the deer posed against fanciful paisley-patterned wall-papers in vivid colors.

"It's amazing," I breathed, unable to look at my husband seated to my right. I knew what he was thinking just by his body language. No way was he going to allow her to mark up her body.

"No color," our daughter assured us. "And I want it right here." She held up the inside of her left arm.

I think my husband gasped before he stuttered, "That can't be safe. I mean there are a lot of veins and what if you needed to give blood or get a line or ..." He seemed to be suppressing his urge to scream, so he was drowning her in a sea of horrific medical scenarios—a way he knew to get at our slightly germ-phobic daughter.

Ever pragmatic, our daughter responded that she had already researched the health risks. She could not give blood for a year. She could not swim or be in chlorine for several weeks after the tattoo. She would need to apply A&D ointment for at least five days, hypoallergenic lotion for another five days after that, or until it stopped peeling or itching. She had to be vigilant about keeping it clean and out of the sun.

"What about a career?" her father asked.

Her goals, which she had set from the very beginning, were to get a BFA in painting, followed by an MFA in painting, so she could teach at the university level and still be a working artist. And, she added, nearly every teacher where she had attended pre-college classes and summer sessions had been inked.

Our daughter had also, to our surprise, done the fieldwork. She had visited every tattoo shop in town, looked at their books, interviewed the artists, and had already decided where she would get it done. She had designed a tattoo for a friend and had gone with him and checked out the cleanliness of the needles and the employees, their professionalism, and their willingness to answer her questions.

In reality, her father and I could do nothing to stop her. She was of legal age. She understood our hesitation, but it was her skin to do with as she pleased.

Eventually, to appease us, she agreed to wait until after our family reunion trip over the summer that would coincide with an eightieth birthday celebration for my father. During this "cooling off period," where my husband hoped she would forget about the idea of a tattoo, an artist friend of ours, who sported a dozen tattoos herself, said to us, "You need to face it: She's going to get this tattoo. This idea is not borne out of a drunken night of partying."

Reluctantly, we agreed. The prejudices against tattoos were ours alone. Our daughter was all the things a parent would want in a child; she had never given us reason to question her decisions. When we returned from vacation, she made an appointment and put down the deposit, and I heard myself saying to her that I wanted to go along.

The appointment was for noon and our friend had advised no caffeine and to make sure she really ate a meal. That morning my daughter arrived downstairs with a nervous stomach and nibbled at a bagel. Because she was slight in frame to begin with, I knew my daughter needed to store some fuel. When she refused, I figured she was having second thoughts. I told her she could back out and forfeit her fifty-dollar deposit. It wouldn't be admitting cowardice.

But it wasn't that she had changed her mind about the tattoo; she was nervous about the pain, considering the sensitive skin inside her left arm. She didn't want to pass out or, worse, be sick to her stomach. She still wanted the tattoo.

By the time we arrived at the tattoo parlor, she had managed to eat a banana and nothing else. One of the guys in the shop told her to take nice deep Lamaze-like breaths, but I could tell her teeth were chattering.

We were ushered into a room. A soft-spoken tattoo artist asked her to take a seat while he donned his black plastic surgical gloves, and then something shifted. She looked relieved as he swabbed the inside of her arm with antibacterial solution. "Are you sure you want the tattoo here? It's a career killer," he said.

I swallowed hard from my seat by her feet, but I said nothing.

"Yes," she answered without hesitation.

As he readied the needle, he asked what the significance was behind the design. I was shocked that of all the things my husband and I *did* want to know, we hadn't asked her this one question. She brought up vegetarianism, her staunch stand on animal rights, which clashed with her fascination with taxidermy. The deer paintings were based on a friend's father's kills. She had spent hours in their basement photographing the deer for many of her paintings. The birds in the antlers, she explained, signified a beginning, an obvious metaphor that I hadn't been paying attention to, so focused was I on the social implications of my daughter's future with a tattoo.

The artist laid a piece of tracing paper with her meticulously drawn deer on the inside of her arm and asked if she liked the placement. She held her arm aloft so I could see the deer's proud torso, the flight of birds that alighted around his antlers and gently flew around the curve of her wrist. A wrist I once could circle with my thumb and forefinger, a wrist I once kissed and tickled.

She gave me a tremulous smile, waiting for my approval. I smiled back. "It's beautiful," I said.

ZOE ZOLBROD

PAI FOOT

N 2010, I PUBLISHED A NOVEL, *CURRENCY,* ABOUT A THAI MAN
and an American woman backpacker who hook up in Thailand and,
in a desperate bid to stay together and score some cash, get involved
in illegal activities. The book is not autobiographical, but I did spend
some time in Thailand in the 1990s, and after my mom read my
novel, she called me. She asked, in a very particular tone – hesitant
and brave and slightly accusatory – "Um, how did you know so much
about what a Thai man would think?"

I had rehearsed for questions like this, and I had decided to be
straightforward.

Now was my chance. "I slept with some of them," I answered.

Mercifully, she didn't ask me for a number. She just said, in
words hung with skepticism: "Are they really that appealing?"

I often feel like a pissy teenager around my mom, and for a
moment I felt myself gathering my resources for a lecture on cul-
tural insensitivity and the reflexive dehumanization of the Other.

You know, something along the lines of: "Well, the word *they* in this context reduces a large number of individual people to a depersonalized mass, and it's impossible to make generalizations on that level ..." But I caught myself, and I gave her the short, true answer: "I thought so."

And the image that came immediately to my mind was not that of my protagonist, with his cascades of black hair and high cheekbones and smooth gold skin spread taut over an inverted *V* of articulated musculature (that a reader of *Currency* would question whether I believed a Thai man could be exceptionally attractive sheds doubt either on my powers of description or on the truism that a reader's inclination is to equate author and narrator), and it was not that of the real-life prototypes from whom he was built. What I saw when I owned up to my predilection for a type was the bottom of a short, wide, maimed foot being held in the air in a bid toward mother-sympathy.

I was in Pai, a little town in the north of Thailand, and I'd just checked in at Riverside Lodge. For a couple of dollars a day, I'd rented one of the two dozen bamboo huts planted in rows next to the Pai River. The managers of this rag-tag accommodation were a couple, a Belgian man and an Australian woman who had just had a baby, and I was standing under the communal palapas talking to the new mom when a young Thai man approached us. Ignoring me, he said, "Look!" to the proprietor, and he held out his foot, which had been pierced in its ball by a thorn.

It was a perfect bloom of a foot – the color of teak, rounded, sturdy yet smooth, free from reddened knobs or yellowed protrusions, its health somehow only enhanced by the circle of black puncture and by the surrounding stain of Mercurochrome. I have never responded so strongly to an isolated body part. The moment is preserved in resin for me; I can hold it out to examine at will. I can feel my tongue contract and the saliva pool beneath it, my words rescind in awe.

Was it the symmetry, some mathematical formula expressed in the concentric circles – ball, stain, hole? Was it the relationship between the colors, in which those exact shades of brown and burgundy scale a perfectly attuned contrast ramp toward the blackest of blacks? The millimeter-sized hole glistened like an iris. Science aside, certainly the posture in which the workaday appendage was held was part of the charm for me. The foot was slipped out of a rubber sandal and lifted waist high while its owner stood firm on the other one. His knee pointed down, his palm cradled the foot top, the foot bottom was leveled as if displaying a cupcake. A class full of experienced yogis would find this pose a wicked hip opener, but under the thatched roof of the palapas it appeared effortless, the wide leg of a fisherman trouser draped just so to reveal a strapping calf. And then there was the attitude: the offering of the foot, the appeal to sympathy and simultaneous lack of self-pity. And the symbolism: Pai was where I became comfortable in Thailand, where I began to identify myself as a traveler – the process might have begun as little as fifteen minutes before – and here was a jungle foot, a thorn puncture, an antiquated medical treatment.

The black pierce appeared to me a portal to a different world. I looked at this guy's foot for what seemed like forever, and I finally pulled back enough to look at him. He had thick black hair cut in a stylish boy-bob, smooth wide cheeks, dense black eyelashes, and black eyes, which I met. I'm sure my desire was absolutely naked, because he looked at me back, and I could almost hear the click of recognition: *low-hanging fruit.*

I'm someone who pays attention to appearances. I stare at people too long. I'm a writer, and I like to deconstruct faces and clothing and the arrangements of limbs, but I also just flat out like pretty ones. Always have. In kindergarten, I wanted to befriend a girl because she had long, inky hair. My earliest memory of visiting the big city of Pittsburgh is sitting in the backseat of our whooshing station wagon and swiveling my head so I could keep the gigantic, billboard-splashed face of a lovely model in sight.

Late to develop in other ways, I was early in discovering my eye for boys. After living elsewhere for a year, I returned to my hometown the summer before sixth grade and studied the yearbook, picking whom I wanted as a boyfriend: Brian Olah, tall and handsome, but distinctively so. I didn't fall for checklist beauty; I had to decide it on my own terms. My relationship with female attractiveness became complicated – I'm unclear whether my concerns led me to or resulted from a feminist consciousness – and I had mixed feelings about my desire to be a pretty girl, how it felt to be treated as one, how concerned the world was with categorizing and policing female appearance. But this never interfered with my appreciation of form. When, catching up, I told a friend about a new beau and slipped in a mention of how good he looked to me, she said, "You always date handsome men. You'll probably marry someone who's not handsome."

"Do you think so?" I said, as if it were an open question. *No way,* I thought. And I was right. Years later, I married that boyfriend. Closing in on two decades together, mired in domestic drudgery, I might be lying if I said not a day goes by, but I'm sure not a week goes by, when his appearance doesn't elicit an almost objective appreciation from me that's distinct from the affection that arises from the familiarity of his features.

But handsome is different than beautiful. Pretty is different than beautiful. Certainly it is in terms of my reaction. I respond to beauty more from a place of helplessness, my ego melting in its beam. It's not like eyes meeting across a room for an exchange of understanding, of human connection; the recognition is not the first move in a game.

A bloom of a foot. A flower. A sunset. The consummation is already past. My response is violent but impersonal. It's not about me. Or I don't want it to be.

The man with the maimed foot was named Ghan. A fledgling trek guide, he lived in one of the bungalows and worked as sort of a houseboy around the place when he was not leading tourists on overnight hikes to hill-tribe villages. Meals were eaten communally at the lodge, and Ghan helped with every step: going to the market, chopping, cooking, serving. Then he sat down to eat with the guests, explaining night after night what was in the jar of sauce being passed: fish sauce, vinegar, chilies; and what to do if the food was too hot: eat plain rice to absorb the oils, don't gulp water that will spread them around.

Of course, I wanted to look at him more, but his presence at dinner pained me. I felt the opposite of flirtatious. I felt shy, so embarrassed by my regard of his person that I wanted to hide my head. Several months earlier, my long-term boyfriend and I had broken up, and I spent the span before I went to Asia doing some rebound gallivanting. I outfitted and paraded myself. Put on red lipstick, red hot pants, shiny vinyl go-go boots. Men responded. But how many of the finer sentiments can you trust when you've waved a red flag at a bull? My trip was supposed to strip away all that. I dressed like an urchin boy. I hacked off my hair. I carried no makeup. I felt ungainly, and although that was part of the point, at that table in Pai I felt almost ashamed by the inequality between Ghan's grace and mine.

But he had my number. It was almost obligatory, the way he tossed lines to me at dinner. The effort felt forced. "Chicago," he called out to me across the table once my hometown had been divulged, "How you like Thai spicy food?" "Chicago, do you want some more?" Or sometimes just: "Chicago!" So I'd look at him and blush. Was he mocking me and my open lust? "Chicago! We're going dancing. You can come."

Ghan, the Belgian expat, and about six of the lodge's guests piled on three motorbikes and buzzed along twisting dark roads to a village festival. Loudspeakers were rigged up to posts surrounding a field, and Thai pop blared to the point of distortion. Ghan politely tried to make conversation with me, leaving me flattered but in agony. We could barely hear each other, and our foreign accents and frames of reference limited even the little we could discern. "Do you want to dance?" he finally shouted at me. "But your foot!" I shouted back. "Sorry. Cannot hear. Better to dance." He hobbled out to the field, and I followed. Then he turned to me and started hopping on one foot, his hair flopping and his trousers shaking to the beat. My own foot pulsed with sympathy for what the movement must be doing to his. "It's okay," I wanted to say. "We don't have to talk. We don't have to dance. It's nice of you to pretend to try, but obviously I'll go to bed with you either way."

But there was no bed in sight. The night was not over. The village festival's offerings neither quaint nor sophisticated enough for backpackers habituated to the cacophony of India and the world-class deejays found down south, we ended up back on the motorbikes, driving farther into the hilly countryside to score some opium.

We pulled up to a small bamboo hut distinguished from those we were renting mostly by the mounds of garlic piled round it. After Ghan and the Belgian muttered negotiations with an awakened resident, we all filed in and a woman emerged from the second room to stoke the fire and hack into it. The man of the house slipped out the door. "To get the opium man," Ghan said. "We wait." The woman didn't meet our eyes. She obviously would have preferred to be sleeping; she obviously hated our presence under her roof. I shriveled. I wondered, *Whose idea was it to come?*

The opium man looked the part: blackened teeth, black fingers, clothes like moss and bark. We took turns depositing money on a pile and lying down face to face with him, our heads resting on pillows of garlic as we accepted the stem of a long pipe whose bowl he tended. He packed it, poked it, kept it lit while we inhaled. At first, it was awkwardness upon the awkwardness, my white bull of a self making the floor shake as I moved toward the pipe, my greedy but unskilled sucking performed within six inches from a face that never met a bar of soap nor tube of Crest.

But, you know, it's opium. It's a great high. And pretty soon there was nothing awkward or uncomfortable at all. There was no need for dancing or repartee and no shame in desire, and when Ghan said, simply, softly, "Zoo, come here and lie with me," I leaped like a gazelle across the room and into his spoon. In between pipes, we kissed. Cushioned, blossoming kisses that lasted – literally, I believe – for hours. People left. The fire went out. I was unaware. When I opened my eyes at dawn, his lashes, against his cheek, were covered with white ash. The curve of the burnished cheek, the echoed curve of the lash, the gentleness of the ash: again with the symphony. The gray light of day only accentuated it. Beauty. And this time I could kiss it. There was more hacking around the fire as others awakened; there was open incivility between the Belgian and the hostess, but it didn't touch me, and somehow Ghan and I were granted our own motorbike. I wrapped my arms around his waist and off we floated through the fog.

We were coupled for the remainder of my time in Pai. We went to the market together, ran errands for the lodge, took scenic motor-bike rides, drank banana milkshakes at cafés. We went to his friends' homes. We spent a lot of time rolling around in my bungalow. It was all so sweet.

But sexy is different than beautiful. Or it can be. It was in this case. One of the things we did together was drive out to the meth-adone clinic, where Ghan got his daily supply and where the clini-cians also tended to his foot.

Pretty much every young man in Pai – or at least every young man a grungy backpacker sleeping with one of them is likely to meet – was on either heroin or methadone. Pai is in poppy country, and this was back when Thailand was still a major producer. Around there, heroin cost practically nothing. Around there, tourism was the only growth industry. Many of the guys worked with backpackers for whom visiting the opium man and smoking white powder out of bamboo bongs was part of the package. And then, of course, we went away, to the beaches or the ruins or the Bangkok sex clubs, to the pot or the X or the mushrooms or the hashish that was the specialty of the next locale. While there the Pai-landers stayed.

Ghan blamed his frequent impotence on the condoms I insisted on, but I suspected otherwise. While his erratic erections would have made me crazy in the past, would have driven me away in a fury of dissatisfaction and self-doubt, it didn't bother me much with him. Nothing did. It was as if I were still high. We cuddled and lounged and explored each other. I loved to look at him. The way his hair swung when he stepped out of his sandals before crossing a threshold, the graceful wrap of his masculine muscles over his delicate frame. Sometimes I held his foot, feigning concern for its injury, wondering at how it could be continually exposed to the elements but remain so plump and fine. Of course, part of it was his youth. He was a tender shoot, bamboo that I could almost see grow. While I was there, he traded the embroidered hill-tribe sash with which he tied his trousers to a Frenchman in return for a logo tee from a windsurfing company, and without his plain white cotton and the smooth fold of fabric around his hips that the sash had allowed him to make, his beauty was shorn just a sliver.

He'd been in Pai for less than a year. Before that, he had been at a monastery, where he had learned English. His family farmed rice. They lived in the jungle, he said. Not close to Pai; somewhere no tourists went. He wanted to take me there to see them. He planned the itinerary: first to Chiang Mai, then on another bus to the closest

town, then three days walking. We would have to wait until his foot
was healed. And then we would have to wait while he led a tourist
trek, so that he'd have some money.

In the meantime, he told me the story of the worst moment of
his life. I feel it would be an invasion to offer it here, but it involved
guarding over a rice field from a platform in the trees on a night
with no moon. I know he gave it to me, the way lovers do, as a gift.

"Not beautiful, but cute, and a very nice person," he told me
drifting off to sleep one night. He sounded like a man who had
recently revaluated his priorities and was pleased with the new order.
Or maybe he was impressed at his ability to achieve accuracy in Eng-
lish. He repeated himself: "Not beautiful, but cute, and a very nice
person." He kissed me.

I accepted this description easily. Unlike compliments earned in
my show-horse stage, it felt like it would last. If he didn't think I was
beautiful, that no longer mattered.

He seemed to me so sweet, so pure: the foot, the heroin, the
methadone, the moonlit rice fields, the Mercurochrome, the monas-
tery. A picturesque vista.

And I thought he was a very nice, too, above-average decent. But
really, how could I know? Upon first acquaintance with a beautiful
person, the existence of any virtue besides it seems such a bounte-
ous gift. Kindness! Wow! And she's so down-to-*earth*! And he's really
funny. And then there's the way beauty affects the taste buds, makes
things seem deliriously sweet even if around the core is bitterness.

Or, at least, it creates delirium for a while. It's the shock of dis-
covery that gives beauty such power. You can reveal it again and
again, of course; it's a living thing, ever changing, moving into

something new. But you can also become accustomed. The balance between Ghan and I shifted. Having started out ashamed, I became almost proud of, certainly I drew confidence from, not being the beautiful one in our pair.

I stayed in Pai longer than I would have otherwise, but not long enough for Ghan's foot to heal completely. Given the offer, I decided to leave with an Australian girl named Vanessa for a less-discovered little town on the Mekong River farther east. Ghan was crestfallen the day I departed. Pouty. He met my eyes only when I roughed out my travel plans and estimated that I might be able to come back around Easter, a word that meant nothing to him. "The beginning of the hot season," I translated. I saw hope flicker.

I did think of him around then. I was in Bangkok. But I didn't have time to get all the way up to Pai before heading off to Kathmandu. I've thought of him many times since, but I spent Easter in Nepal.

M.J. FIEVRE

THE
OTHER
PAPA

Jeweled chopsticks and flowered pins lie scattered on the vanity top. Mother's hair is up in an elaborate bun with languorous permed curls dangling along the sides of her face. Sitting on the bed, Papa watches her as she clasps her pearl necklace closed.

Papa is too far to hold me, too close to ignore, and when I reach over to him, bouncing the mattress, he takes my hand—just for a second or two. Then he lets go.

"My sister is visiting tonight," Mother says.

I'm holding a bottle of perfume found on the night table. I douse Papa's *Le Troisième Homme* on my wrist and neck, the underside of my arms, rubbing in my father's musky scent like a salve.

"I don't want to see anyone," Papa says.

He is whispering. His nightly theatrics have ravaged his vocal chords. He's been yelling again—a mean, volatile storm.

"But it's Mom's birthday," I say.

A faint smile reveals a dimple in Mother's right cheek. "It is, isn't it?" she says.

Usually, Papa enjoys parties. He gets swept up in the festivity, becomes animated, involved, telling funny anecdotes, invariably getting the biggest laughs of the evening. But he's the Other Papa today. I can tell he's suddenly in one of his moods. His eyebrows join together in a frown line across his forehead. His thin face is stern, lips latched tight.

You see, one day my father is normal, calm, quiet, in control, reliable; the next he becomes a wild-eyed stranger, screaming so loud that my ears sting.

Mother says he has mood swings.

One of Mother's hairs falls out of her curl; a piece of her life is gone without a sound. Outside, neighbors shriek out front doors, brakes squeal – people's afternoons are unfolding. The November sun beats against the window, bounces off Mother's vanity mirror. Shadows fall across the carpet, elongating.

I can see my reflection in the vanity mirror. It is frightening to see Papa stare at me from my own face. I have his eyes, his ears, and the line of his jaw. Just like his, my shoulders are hunched in that good-natured, non-threatening way. A deception – my father is rangy, temperamental, twitchy with impatience.

Both my parents are beautiful. Papa has an epicene quality that lends him a youthful air, even as he slips into middle age. Mother is witty and tender. His voice booms; hers tinkles like tiny bells. As for me, my acne is flourishing – I wear it with wounded pride, as though my scars hold a secret that others can't really appreciate.

I try to tell a joke to make Papa happy. "*Tim Tim*," I start, leaning over his shoulder. Knock-knock.

"Quiet!" he yells, shrugging off my embrace.

He was supposed to say, "*Bwa sèch*." My mother turns and glares. I'm sure Papa hates me. I want to break out of the room, out of the hostile air that fills its every corner. But the more I try to *pouf*, disappear, the more present I feel, until, exhausted, I give in, float with Papa's angry words. If I don't, I might drown with and in these words. If I don't, these words might become my own–etched in my brain, and later released from my mouth.

WHEN AUNT G KISSES ME SHE LEAVES LIPSTICK ON MY CHEEKS. She measures my every inch because it helps her feel the flow of time, and she shakes her head as if it makes her sad. "Oh, my! We're not getting any younger, Tita, are we? My, oh my, can you believe how fast they grow?"

Papa finally agreed to the party. He's always changing his mind for no apparent reason.

Aunt G hugs me. "You're so beautiful," she says. "Looking more and more like your father."

My mother shoots her a strange look–something like sorrow; the look you'd have if you were helpless to save your daughter. Maybe Mother worries I might become my father, rageful with misery. Maybe she's aware of the anger sluicing through me sometimes–it can be there at the end of a sentence, startling even me like a shadow slinking by an open door. Who knows? I might explode one day. In the morning, when the sun rises, mean as a snake, even before my first thought is shaped, there is this thumping in my heart, like a ticking clock. Something inside me wants to be released. I want to reach in, grab it, and punch it against the wall. And I also want to yell–but I can't. Because I can't allow myself to become my father.

Papa … No one can defeat him at dominoes. Crowded around the table, the adults whoop and holler. Drinks sit away from elbows. Bids are made. My mother yells, "Ha-ha!" Aunt G grins. Papa laughs. The cookie plate for the children is never empty. The radio is on. Toto Bissainthe is singing to Papa Damballah, the voodoo god.

"Dance with me," Papa says.

My father swoops and grabs my shoulders and I'm laughing as we spin. One foot hits the table with a dull sudden thump and my mother says, "Honey!" but I can only see her sometimes in the green blur of the kitchen. *Nou vire, vire, vire.* We turn, and turn, and turn.

"Honey, you're making her dizzy," Mother says.

When Papa stops, he's smiling. He pulls me into a tight arm-breaking hug and then I am free. My stomach rolls and lurches and I beam at my father who laughs at me. I am the happiest and most loved girl there ever was. I am better than anyone.

I show everyone the tooth I lost–yellow and ugly. Pitted and scarred and smooth, too. With a jagged head and a fang of a root.

Sometimes I feel like a yellow tooth inside. But not right now, when Papa is laughing again.

"Too much sugar," Aunt G says disapprovingly, opening her mouth wide so we can see all her white teeth and her tongue, the end of her tongue, a small red bulb wobbling in the dark vault beneath her palate. She looks at me seriously. "No more candy for you, *made-*

moiselle. You're so beautiful—you don't want to become a toothless *dan rachòt.*"

Mother cooked all afternoon, and the fragrance of roasting ham, garlic, and other spices, the family milling around, laughing and talking, makes it like Christmas. My sister Patricia and I switch on the TV, fiddle with the knobs and the antenna until the horizontal lines disappear and we can watch *Languichatte,* the Haitian comedy show. We sink to the floor cross-legged, our eyes on the screen. The sound of laughter mingles with the hissing of steaming kettles, the clink of silverware on plates, and the bell-like tones of glasses touching each other in a salute to peace.

My mother sighs, warm and filled with contentment. My father groans, for he has eaten too much and dessert is still to come.

THE OTHER PAPA IS BACK.

Hours after the party, Mother, my sister, and I have locked ourselves in my parents' bedroom because Papa is in a rage.

"It will be better if you open the door, Tita," Papa says from behind the door. "I don't want to force my way in."

Patricia puts her hands over her ears, speaking softly to herself, shaking so hard I want to tie her down. Mother begs Papa—through the door—to calm down. The pounding stops for a few minutes or so and then begins again. "Open up, Tita, or so help me God, I'll break the door down. Tita!" The name seems to belong to someone else, even though it is Papa's voice calling it. A very angry voice.

My mother grimaces when she touches her eye, and the skin is turning several different colors. I'm afraid my father will break the door down. He is still out there. He's back to calling her name. "Tita. Tita. Let me in. Let. Me. In."

Pound. Pound. Pound.

I grab a book and throw it the door. "Go away! I hate you."

Mother takes my hand. "Don't be like that." Her other hand is on her temple and she's gazing out at nothing. I see a tear roll down the silhouette of her shadowed cheek.

Then he begins rattling the doorknob with one hand and banging at the wood with the other. The floor is going to swallow me. The bedroom walls start caving in. The rough spots on the carpet are bloody footprints and dark creatures from the corners of the room bob their huge heads as they weave and glide closer.

"Open the *fucking* door," Papa says.

"Mom?" I say, touching her shoulder.

She rubs her face and turns to look at me. "I bet I look a mess," she says.

"You're still pretty," I whisper. "Even with snot on your nose."

"Oh, honey," she says wetly. She takes us both in her arms, and her face is damp against our cheeks. Her fingers stroke our heads.

The doorknob turns clockwise, rattles, and quickly turns counterclockwise. Mother wedges a chair under the doorknob. She and I lean with all our might against the door, but we're losing the battle. There are two of us (my sister is too terrified), but a very angry man is pushing the door from the other side. Papa throws his entire body weight into a running tackle that starts at the other end of the hallway and ends with a splintering *ka-blam* at the bedroom door.

Suddenly, our resistance proves too feeble and the door collapses inward, sending Mother and me sprawling, crashing the chair into the wall. Papa falls against the vanity–jeweled chopsticks and flowered pins fly to the ground. In an attempt to steady himself, he knocks over a small mirror and suddenly there is blood everywhere.

In an instant, Papa is over the rage–just like that. He will say later that the pain brought back lucidity. He sits on the bed, dumbfounded. "What am I doing?"

My reflection stares at me from the broken mirror on the floor–and for the first time I can see my mother somewhere in that face. Mother–kind-hearted and shy, far from unmanageable. I don't have to be *that* child–savage and feral, overwhelmed by some fury boiling inside me. It is true that what's born in me lies still for now, until I am grown and find my way. But only time will tell: that dormant nature might be something calm and loving–truly beautiful, like Mother.

STEPHEN WALTER

UPLAND FALL

September and the streamside ash
Gleams yellow in the afternoon;
They drowsily behold the flash
Of leaves against dark water, soon

Forgotten as they pass below
The ridgeline's overarching green;
Lulled by resinous air they slow,
Then touch and shed their clothes unseen

Then sleep embowered in white pine.
Brushing needles from her sleeve
He says, I've never seen so fine
An early fall. Please stay. Don't leave

Me in these mountains on my own,
Not now before the leaves have turned;
To wander the bright paths alone
Would be too much to bear. I yearned

For you all summer, now you're here:
Why ruin splendor at its start?
At night the golden star shines clear;
He knows that she will soon depart.

October and the tupelo
Ignites into a glossy blaze;
Uphill the dogwood is aglow
With scarlet drupes set in a haze

Of dusky red as she lies slack,
Half-sleeping, head upon his arm.
He traces curves along her back
With a stray leaf; the days run warm

But mornings clot with mist until
At dawn their bare feet slide on frost;
A week of rain drives in its chill
As if in grief at ripeness lost,

Then evening takes them unawares
With sudden brightness as the sky
Clears to reveal the waning flares
Of silver maples lit up by

A parting ray against dark cloud
Like water sun-flecked over rocks,
And gusting winds flush waves of loud
Birds, scattering the migrant flocks

Like leaves as twilight turns to red.
November brings the bleakest fog,
A film of ashes in his bed.
He sickens at brown leaves that clog

The ditch downstream from a bur oak;
No birds sing in the bare-stripped tree.
He dwells upon the words she spoke:
We love the season best when we

Forget where it is heading.
Splendor has no start, she said, or chance
To stay; no use in dreading
What fades already at each glance.

What he dreads now are colder sights
Like bloody feathers on fresh snow,
Desolation of the Long Nights
Moon shining on dead twigs, the slow

Paralysis of brittle winter
Light, stubble fields strewn with decay.
He wonders if he dreamed of her,
Yet feels she left him anyway.

GREG OLEAR

THE LINE
WAVER

THE GARISH GLASS MONSTROSITY DIRECTLY ABOVE THE FRONT door of a typical McMansion – its distinguishing feature – is called a Palladian window. Although in the real estate patois McMansions are known as Colonials, the Palladian window is a more recent innovation, re-popularized by the so-called Adam style of the Victorian period.

I know this because my son, Dominick, is interested in architecture, and we often read a dense tome called *A Field Guide to American Houses*. When we come to the Adam houses (named, incidentally, for the brother architects who popularized them, and not the orchard thief of Biblical renown), I tell my son that I abhor the style, because of the distinctive Palladian window.

"Why?" he asks, as five-year-olds will.

I find this a difficult question to answer. I could respond that I find Palladian windows aesthetically ugly, but, while true, that isn't really why I detest them. Or I could blame my aversion on their lack of utility; vestiges of French doors, Palladian windows have lost their function with their balcony and are, in modern houses, giant panes of glass illuminating unused upstairs alcoves. But there are plenty of not-very-useful features in other kinds of houses that I do like – the exaggerated roof of the French Eclectics, say. So that isn't it, either.

"Why, Daddy?"

I decide to cop out, as fathers will. "I just don't," I tell him.

But Dominick's question gnaws at me.

THE RECORDING ENGINEER LARS FOX MADE AN INTERESTING remark to *Rolling Stone* magazine a few years back.

"If you're fifteen," he said, "you've probably never heard a shitty drum performance."

While there is certainly less-than-stellar percussion work on the airwaves, he makes a good point.

Back in the day, when Roy Orbison or Johnny Cash or Elvis Presley went into a studio, engineers recorded their respective bands playing the songs together live. Whole albums were laid down over long weekends. Drummers did not even wear click-track headphones. There was very little post-production. If someone sucked, they sucked – there was no place to hide.

This is no longer the case. Skipped beats can be repaired. Tempos can be shifted. Flubbed notes can be erased. Wavering vocals can be corrected. And in an increasingly intricate mastering process, recordings are compressed to be as loud as possible without losing integrity (which is why when you play an Elton John CD after an Amy Winehouse CD, you have to jack up the volume).

The result, as Lars astutely pointed out, is this: Every piece of music we hear is technically perfect.

A HUMAN BEING, IT'S SAID, CANNOT DRAW A PERFECT CIRCLE FREE-hand. We all know intuitively what a circle is, but without the aid of a compass—and even with a compass, is a penciled-in figure really 100% accurate?—we cannot replicate one.

But with Photoshop, I can render a perfect circle at will.

A CENTURY AND A HALF AGO – THE YEAR THE CIVIL WAR began—most of the technology we take for granted did not exist. Cameras were rudimentary and expensive. The railroad had just begun its ascendancy. Medicine was a joke. There were no "moving pictures," no color photographs, no glossy magazines, no television, no radio, no automobiles or highways on which to drive them, no airplanes, telephones, or Internet. There was not much appreciable difference between life in 1860 and life in 1760, or 1660, or even 1560.

How long would it take for a boy entering puberty in 1860 to see the undressed body of an attractive woman? There were more paintings than photographs of nudes, and those paintings hung in museums far, far away, so our boy would have to catch a glimpse of an actual flesh-and-blood female. If he didn't spy on girls at a swimming hole, or visit a brothel, he might not feast his eyes on the feminine form in all its glory until the day he got married (or the day he knocked up the girl he would be forced at gunpoint to marry).

And if he did get lucky and beheld a bathing beauty, what would she look like? What are the chances that she would be pretty, even by 1860 standards? And in what scenario could he drink in that image at his leisure, unconcerned about being caught *in flagrante delicto*, like that mythological deer in the headlights, Actaeon? Chances are, our pubescent boy will live his entire life and witness precious few ladies *en déshabillé*.

I just typed in "naked celebrities" on Google and was led to a site called Celebrity Pink, on which are images of Kim Kardashian fornicating with Ray J; the beautiful bare bosoms of Charlize Theron, Rihanna, and Megan Fox; and Paris Hilton, Britney Spears, and Lindsay Lohan with mouths full of metonymical manhood.

Not only do I have unfettered access to images of female nudes, the nudes are doing things that would have made our Civil War–era lad blush. And they are all drop-dead gorgeous.

Perfect women at my DSL'd fingertips.

MCMANSIONS ARE, OBJECTIVELY SPEAKING, NICE PLACES TO LIVE. They offer every amenity a fairly well-off American could ask for: plenty of square footage, a flowing floor plan, ample storage space, walk-in closets, three-car garages, Jacuzzi tubs, lofted ceilings, fireplaces, central air conditioning. All the corners are square; all the walls are level; all the doors are squeakless. These houses are a sort of Greatest Hits of architecture, appropriating the best that each style has to offer: Great room. Open entryway with circular staircase. Bonus room. Palladian window.

These are not just better homes; they are perfect ones.

A STAPLE OF THE MIMI FEROCIOUS BAND'S LIVE SET IS THEIR rousing cover of "I Feel Love." My wife belts out these high notes, clear and loud and perfectly in tune, the drums pound out a hot beat, and the bassist, David Wilson, cranks out a line that, in the original Donna Summer version, is synthesized because it's so hard to play.

I've watched them do that song hundreds of times, and David never messes up. Once, he broke a string – no small feat on a bass – and still managed to play the song flawlessly, transposing on the fly. An incredible performance.

On the Mimi Ferocious recording, though, strong as the track is, something gets lost in translation. David is doing the same thing, the notes are the same, the playing is still top-notch.

So what's changed? My ears. Because it's a CD, I don't pay any attention to the degree of difficulty. When I listen to an album, I expect – I demand – perfection. Like baseball umpires, it's only when something goes awry that I notice.

THE AMOUNT OF SKILL THAT IS REQUIRED OF A SYMPHONY orchestra's first violinist to tackle a challenging piece of music, the years of rigorous training to get the instrument to sound just so – nothing on Earth grates on the ears as hideously as a violin in the hands of someone who does not know how to play – the dedication and devotion and discipline are staggering to contemplate.

And where do most of us hear the aural fruit of all that labor? In elevators. In dentists' lobbies. In telephones, as we wait for customer service.

Even our background noise is perfect.

THE ARTIST MARGARET KILGALLEN (1967 – 2001) HAD A THING FOR hand-painted signs. She would scour ramshackle storefronts in the poorer sections of cities – establishments that could not afford slick, professional print jobs and instead produced their own. These signs she incorporated into her work.

As the stone the builders rejected became the cornerstone for the church, so Kilgallen found beauty in flaws.

Kilgallen said in an interview with PBS,

[I]n my own work, I do everything by hand. I don't project or use anything mechanical, because even though I do spend a lot of time trying to perfect my line work and my hand, my hand will always be imperfect because it's human. And I think it's the part that's … interesting, that even if I'm doing really big letters and I spend a lot of time going over the line and over the line and trying to make it straight, I'll never be able to make it straight. From a distance it might look straight, but when you get close up, you can always see the line waver. And I think that's where the beauty is.

Her art is about rejection of perfection. She was onto something.

HEIDI PRATT NÉE MONTAG, THE VILLAINESS A FEW SEASONS removed from MTV's reality show *The Hills*, might not have a good head on her shoulders, but she's always had a good-looking one.

Whatever you can say for her other talents—and the less said the better—Heidi is hot. Heidi in high school was about as pretty as pretty gets. This has not stopped her from getting plastic surgery a whopping ten times, which seems excessive for anyone, particularly a naturally stunning beauty of twenty-three.

Pulchritude is not enough; Pratt wants perfection.

What she does not realize is that our attitude toward perfection is in flux.

ARTISTS TRADITIONALLY TOOK TO THE COUNTRY FOR INSPIRATION. Van Gogh at Arles, Monet at Giverny, Gauguin in Tahiti, Pollock in East Hampton.

Kilgallen lived on the Lower East Side of New York in the early 1990s, when the Lower East Side was sketchy if not outright dangerous. Before that, she lived in San Francisco.

Today, artists are associated not with bucolic countrysides but with revitalization of blighted cities. Case in point: Beacon, NY. Once an industrial city known for manufacturing hats, Beacon went south when men stopped wearing them. Economic freefall and urban decay ceased only when the artists came. Dia: Beacon, the town's modern art museum that features installations too large for most exhibit spaces, is located in what used to be a Nabisco factory.

Artists are the Cassandras of real estate. They are visionaries, able to find beauty in ugliness.

TIME WAS, CLEAN, CRISP DUNGAREES SMACKED OF MONEY AND style. Only men who did not work the fields could keep their jeans looking perfect.

Now Heidi Pratt and the rest of the fashionable set pay big money for jeans that are discolored, faded, torn.

Furniture, too, comes "distressed." New tables and chairs and chests of drawers are manufactured to look like odd pieces found at antique shops in Hudson, NY (another formerly fallen city revitalized by artists).

The stuff that is the shiniest – the stuff our Civil War child would pick for his McMansion – is usually shit.

ARCHITECTURE MIRRORS CULTURE. THE HOUSES WE CHOOSE TO build speak to our hopes, our aspirations, our desires. Their windows (Palladian or otherwise) are looking glasses in which are reflected our societal values.

McMansions project flawlessness: the triumph of mechanical construction over the shaky human hand, the luxury of precision. Monuments to success and achievement, to the conquest of mistakes, they are intended to wow. But the wow they now elicit carries a different connotation than what their builders intended.

Somewhere along the line, we have shifted paradigms. We have adopted Kilgallen's aesthetic. We have begun to reject the perfect. We now find beauty in wavering lines. In human fallibility. In flaws.

Consequently, McMansions have become a symbol of decadence, of surfeit, of the tyranny of homogeneity. One can imagine

Ozymandias staring out a Palladian window with his sneer of cold command, lording it over the poor suckers in their split-levels and raised ranches and Cape Cods. Look on my works, ye mighty, and despair! Nothing remains but foreclosure notices and unpaid heating bills.

And this, my son, is the answer to your question. It's not the Palladian window itself that I find an abomination but what it represents: soulless, cold, inhuman perfection.

ELIZABETH COLLINS

BEHELD, BEHOLDEN

THE SKY HANGS LOW, THICKLY PAPERED WITH CLOUDS. IT IS summer, but the weather feels slightly cool. The air is wet. It is midafternoon. Play time.

WHAT RELEASE DOES A FIVE-YEAR-OLD GIRL, ONE OFTEN STUFFED into starchy, hand-smocked dresses, find in wearing blue jeans and a unisex-looking navy blue T-shirt? She feels tough, together, in control of herself for once. The outfit is finished off with a pair of strappy, white sandals, a little-girl staple and a nod to femininity in summertime.

Flying down the stairs, over thick celadon carpet, heading for the door.

Wait, where are you going? asks her mother.

To Jessica and Paul's house.

Wait—what are you wearing? The mother is not visible, is somewhere in the kitchen, perhaps hurriedly drying her hands on a dish towel.

The five-year-old girl freezes. She doesn't want to get into this; she just wants to leave.

What are you wearing? the question comes again. The mother comes to check. A critical glance; her mouth curls in disapproval.

Elizabeth, you've got on dark blue pants with a dark blue shirt!

Yes. It matches. Right?

It looks like a jail uniform! Go put something else on. Please!

Do I have to?

No, but … it looks bad. If you don't care what you're wearing …

I don't care. I like these clothes.

The little girl runs out, goes off to play with her young neighbors. The screen door bangs shut behind her. The girl's long, wavy brown hair flies—free and barely brushed—in the wind.

EVERYTHING IS SHINY HERE AT THE JACKSON'S HOUSE. THE WALLpaper has spots of foil intertwined in areas of fuzzy, olive-green leaves. Nice to rub with fingertips, to see your hopeful, eager face reflected in the tiny mirrors.

There are books full of metallic wallpaper samples for crafting. Cut with scissors. Paste.

Boys and girls play happily together, then disband. Boys ride Big Wheels and bicycles in the driveway. Girls keep playing with the pretty paper.

Mrs. Jackson has been consumed with redecorating her ranch house. The foyer near the front door is tiled with small squares that look like tiger's-eye jewelry.

THE FIVE-YEAR-OLD GIRL WALKS QUICKLY TO THE FRONT DOOR. She plans to call to the boys outside. Tease them. But suddenly, she slips on the tiny tiger's-eye tiles, swirled as they are in variegated shades of brown, yellow, amber.

The flat soles of her girlish white sandals send her flying, crashing into what she'll later be told was a porcelain umbrella stand.

The girl watches herself fall, as if from a distance. She hears the crash rather than feels it, sees the shards of white china that lie all around her. She feels no pain yet, only wonder. What just happened? What is broken? Did she break it?

A warm pool of blood seeps quickly from her face, encircling her body on the floor. The blood feels soft and deep and almost luxurious. It almost feels as if she is swimming in it.

Oh! My! God! Pick her up! Get her over here.

Use these towels.

Get more towels. Hurry!

Press them to her face.

Get her in the sink. Carry her to the sink. Put her head in the sink!

Call her parents.

No, go and get them. Jessica, go and get them. Tell them there's been an accident.

Come back! Get back here! Help me.

She won't stop bleeding!

THE NEXT THING THE GIRL KNOWS, SHE IS SITTING IN THE BACK of her parents' Volkswagen, going to the hospital.

It doesn't hurt, Daddy.

That's good, Princess, he replies calmly. Warmly. Hold that towel to your nose, okay? Just keep holding it there.

The girl does as she is told, but then she feels a sudden curiosity. What is wrong with her nose, anyway? What does it look like? She peels the blood-soaked tea towel away, cranes her neck to see into the rearview mirror.

Don't do that! Don't look at it! Her father is shouting now. Is he mad?

The girl nearly faints from the sight of her face, cleanly torn open. Sliced from the corner of her left eye, all the way down the side of her nose, cut straight across her nostrils. Dark red with blood. Darker inside.

The wound is like a ripped envelope advertising its contents. Horrifying.

WHAT HAPPENS NEXT? THE GIRL RECALLS ONLY HOW SHE IS quickly wheeled down hallways on a gurney. Doors, elevators, flickering fluorescent lights flip past her, like images drawn by an animator. Looming, masked faces look down on her. Strangers speak soothingly.

She briefly sees her mother swooning nearby in the hallway. She hears her father calling for *smelling salts*.

What are smelling salts? Sounds disgusting. Ooh, smells worse.

Then she hears, *Plastic surgeon, plastic surgeon. We're going to need the best plastic surgeon. Who's the best? We need that one.*

The girl doesn't even know what a plastic surgeon is, but it sounds serious. She is still in no pain, still in shock. She thinks only, *But I'm not made of plastic…*

CUT HER CLOTHES OFF.

Several pairs of frighteningly large shears rip into her favorite jeans, shred her T-shirt, ruin her outfit. The girl watches as the scissors cut close to her flesh. Her eyes widen. Is this happening to her? Is this real?

Now she is lying on a steel table, clad only in white cotton underpants flocked with tiny pink rosebuds. She is cold. Humiliated.

Should I give it to her in the ass?

In the ass? *Ass* is a bad word. Who said that? A bad person.

A nurse with short brown hair is holding a large hypodermic. The nurse's head swivels, questioning unseen authorities. She nods, then plunges the needle into the little girl's thigh.

The plastic surgeon arrives. The girl is not sure how much time has passed. But here is Dr. Leonardo, a name she will long remember.

The surgeon surveys the damage to the little girl's nose and, without comment, sets to work. He's a fix-it man. His voice is soft.

Dr. Leonardo likes classical music playing while he works. He enjoys humming. He also seems to enjoy hospital gossip.

A bevy of nurses cluster around him, vying for his attention, so close, so close. The nurses are like twittering birds – chickadees, perhaps. They are like groupies surrounding David Cassidy, or just somebody they revere and want to impress.

Dr. Leonardo cleans and sews, and they all gossip about some people they know – some other nurse, some other doctor – who have been "getting it on."

The girl wonders what this means. Getting what on? Getting on what?

Dr. Leonardo plucks all the pieces of porcelain out of her skin. This hurts, and it seems to go on forever. Then, he lies. *Oh, here's a big piece of porcelain, last one!* He doesn't even tell the girl that he is anesthetizing her nose with needles. She whimpers.

YOUR DAUGHTER ALMOST LOST HER NOSE. WHEN I FIRST SAW IT, I thought, "There is nothing I can do to save that nose." It was barely on her face anymore.

Dr. Leonardo is talking to her mother. He sounds mildly annoyed, but maybe this is because the girl's mother – and the girl does not understand this at all; it seems so weird – is pulling on his sleeve and weeping, begging, pleading, asking over and over, *What will she look like now? Will she still be pretty?*

A thin, white line. That's what the doctor is saying the scar will look like if – and this is key – the little girl's skin is properly protected while it heals. Dr. Leonardo keeps explaining about the thin, white line.

Use vitamin E. A sunhat. Put a Band-Aid over the scar whenever she's in the sun. That scar can get no sun.

What about swimming?

Not for a couple of weeks. But then, fine. Remember! No sun on the scar. Cover the scar at all times.

The mother finally seems to understand.

THE GIRL IS DRIVEN HOME. FIRST, THOUGH, A STOP AT THE DRUG-store for vitamin E. Tylenol. Hershey bars. Ice cream.

She gets into her parents' bed. She is happy with the treats and attention. She feels like jumping on the bed, but this is not allowed.

Ring!! goes the phone. *Ring!! Ring!!*

Everyone who calls wants to know the same thing: *How many stitches?*

The girl wonders about this herself. She touches – gingerly, unsure – the long line of fuzzy black sutures. They cling to the side of her nose like a hairy caterpillar. They are ugly. Her nose feels at once tender and numb.

It's rude to ask how many stitches. Can you believe people keep ask-ing that? Her mother is talking to her father, still shaken, still – it seems – on the verge of crying. She says, almost mournfully, This would have to happen when Elizabeth was wearing that terrible outfit.

The girl's mother believes in dressing up for doctors. Even though they always make you take your clothes off. Even though the clothes the girl had on before ended up in the garbage.

The parents confer for a minute and then sneak up on the lit-tle girl, sporting fake grins, like Halloween masks. One holds a glass of water, one a large, translucent yellow capsule. *You have to swal-low this*, they say. The girl shakes her head no. The capsule is *gigantic*.

Her mother and father try to teach her how to swallow a pill. The girl cries. There's no way. She doesn't want to try it. It's frighten-ing. Water runs down the girl's chin; the capsule ends up somewhere in the middle of her throat, pointing out through her pale skin like a lump, a stone.

The mother's voice rises, quavers. *This is important. You need to do this. The doctor said so.*

There is also a bottle of vitamin E oil that has a little brush inside, like nail polish. The oil gets brushed onto the girl's nose twice a day. What is vitamin E, anyway, the girl wonders? A vitamin for emergencies?

Appearances obviously matter. Appearances reflect on the person in charge. If it looks good, perhaps people will think it *is* good.

The girl does not know where this philosophy originated, if it was borne out of the times when her mother's home was surprise inspected to see if she was worthy enough to adopt a child.

The mother might simply be a product of her generation, one that came of age in the late 1950s and early 1960s—a generation that says mothers should always make sure that their daughters look nice. Girls should wear a ribbon in their hair. Dinner really ought to be on the table every night by six.

Wiping at some dust balls in the corner, the mother says she wants her house to *look* clean. She says she doesn't care if it actually *is* clean.

The mother sews fancy clothes and knits sweaters with elaborate blackberry and basketweave stitches. She weaves wreaths out of found pinecones, and embroiders complex, pastoral scenes with curly fleeced sheep, vivid flowers, rushing rivers.

She spends hours kneading, braiding, baking, and glazing fat, glossy loaves of challah bread. Her daughter aches with hunger, smelling the baking bread, watching it cool on the counter. But this bread is not for eating; no, instead, the mother hangs these shiny loaves of bread *on the wall*. They hang for years, until they crumble.

Their house is bedecked with these carefully made objects. Giant jars of olives, and gifts of homemade jam (some that the girl made herself) adorn an open shelf in the kitchen, plaid bows gracing their fat, crystal necks.

These things are for appearances. These beautiful, useless objects are for public display. They exist only to make an impression: *Look how homey it is here, how pretty.*

THE GIRL GROWS OLDER. HER MOTHER TELLS HER THAT SHE needs to wear some makeup. When the girl leaves the house bare-faced, her mother says, *You look like death warmed over. You need some blush, some lipstick.*

It is deeply ironic that the girl's mother says this because she barely wears makeup. She cares little about such things, and even washes her face with Irish Spring.

When she looks at herself, the mother sees nothing wrong. When she looks at her daughter, she thinks: *Her hair could be neater. She always looks so terribly pale.*

A pretty girl should live up to expectations, says the mother. If one has the capacity to be pretty, then one should be—no excuses—perpetually attractive. A gift, such as beauty, should be used and appreciated, not taken for granted.

The girl learns all this, but years later, she still does her own thing. She looks the way she looks. She brushes her hair, but doesn't obsess over it, and refuses to use "product" if it makes her hair feel sticky. She wears makeup, but only a little of the very best makeup, artfully applied after much study of technique, so that it looks natural.

No matter what, however, she hears in her mind the muttered admonitions: *You should cover up that scar with makeup. If only you hadn't run away screaming when Dr. Leonardo was going to do the dermabrasion.*

I'd like to see you lie still while a masked man comes toward your face with a belt sander, the girl said in reply once, and that ended the hounding.

The girl doesn't see her own scar anymore. Funny how that is. Some people still ask her about it, which is always jarring, but to her, the scar is not an issue. It is simply there, as if it has always been there.

There are other questions, though, also having to do with appearance, also annoying and closer to home: *Why don't you buy an elegant, expensive overcoat? You need a very special, very pretty couch. Custom-made. Don't you agree? And when are you going to have a beautiful house, a showplace?*

Her mother doesn't have to say these things. The girl, fully grown now but still a child in her own memory, will always – despite not caring about such superficial things – always hear them.

J.E. FISHMAN

SPINNING

THIS IS THE STORY OF THE MOST BEAUTIFUL SERVE I EVER hit in my life.

I should begin by noting that I didn't learn to hit a tennis ball with any significant degree of competence until my mid-thirties. That isn't to say that I'd never hit a tennis ball before.

Like many American males, balls featured prominently in my childhood: footballs, handballs, paddle balls, baseballs. I was a casual athlete, though. We played football in the street, other forms of pickup games in the park. I dropped out of Little League baseball as soon as a boy could retreat with his self-respect intact, around the age of nine or ten.

In the sixth-grade schoolyard, I managed for a brief period to lead the charge in touch football and in softball. But that was an uncouth kind of accomplishment, based more on moxie than refined skill. My mother was dying at home. Perhaps, perversely, that gave me a sharp edge for a while.

In junior high, I had an abbreviated and useless stint on the JV soccer field as a scrub goalie. If I played a quality minute, I don't remember it.

Basketball became my sport. I was tall and lanky and learned to jump shot from Rick Barry, the only player to hold seasonal scoring titles in the NCAA, ABA, and NBA. Barry played for the Nets, and a friend of our family was one of the team owners. I made frequent visits to the locker room and after one team practice Barry gave me a few pointers. We had a hoop in the backyard, where I spent hours a day working on my release. At the new county park, games came together spontaneously, often involving overweight older players. I learned how to use my hip and fight for position. I learned how to put my shoulder and elbow into drives to the hoop. I learned to head fake. But on the school team, I was a sixth man, contributing no more than a few baskets per game.

For most of my life, tennis followed a similar pattern. The lessons I received were catch-as-catch can and rarely within the context of an organized youth program. As a teenager, I hacked around with my father's old aluminum Head racket, an implement with a tiny face and a thick red plastic neck. Although my father had become an avid tennis player – or maybe because of that fact, to differentiate myself – I confined my tennis to games at the park with friends who took the sport no more seriously than I did. My sneakers rarely brushed the green Har-Tru of Inwood Country Club, where we were members.

Flashes of semi-competence arose, however, and one of them came at that very club. There was a youth tennis tournament that I agreed to play at my father's urging. As it turned out, only one other player had entered in my age group, so the only match we played became the final. My opponent was a character I didn't know well, not a friend. The club had been founded – or, at least, brought to local prominence – by Jews of German descent, formal people who held themselves above those with more questionable pedigrees. This kid's grandfather had been one of those club builders while our family had joined only a couple of years before. Never mind that my father ran his own successful accounting firm and earned every penny in his pocket. This kid wore polo shirts with the collar turned up and attended private school. I went to public school and looked the part. He took lessons every Saturday and worked on his tennis game. I was the scrapper perfecting his lay-up, never his serve. It shouldn't have been any contest at all, which of course is what made things interesting. I won the first set and might have won the second if I'd wanted it half as much as my opponent. The third he took going away, but I've never seen anyone look so miserable in victory. After all, he should have creamed my ugly game from the outset.

Fifteen years later, I'd done nothing to add to the legend. When I lived in Manhattan, I kept in shape playing racquetball but rarely lifted a tennis racket, other than the occasional lesson or hack-around on vacation. In my late twenties, however, my wife and I moved to Bedford in Westchester County. The old house we bought had a rundown tennis court, which inspired me to pick up the stick more in earnest. At the suggestion of a friend, I joined a health facility in nearby Mt. Kisco called the Saw Mill Club and began to participate in an evening tennis league. One day, I was standing at the plate-glass window, looking down at a game, when a person on the court missed an easy shot and dropped his racket in frustration. An acquaintance, John, said next to me, "That guy's been playing for twenty years and making the same mistakes over and over. How does he expect to get any better if he never works on his game?" He was right. I started taking lessons and I got better—but incrementally, not dramatically.

Then, a couple years later, I looked down from the same window and saw John having a lesson with a new pro across the net. This pro didn't look like the other pros I'd used. His racket didn't so much meet the ball as flow through it. He was a big guy—six-four—but he moved with balance and gracefulness. Not that he scrambled around much. From the moment he dropped a ball from his right hand and started the rally with a flick of the other wrist, every step had assurance behind it and every stroke came with fluidity and purpose.

I TURNED TO SOMEONE STANDING BESIDE ME. "WHO IS THAT?"

He said the pro's name was Rob. I pressed him for more details and he explained that Rob was taking a break from the professional tennis tour, teaching some lessons while he rehabilitated an injured shoulder.

I stood awestruck. "I need this guy."

The man next to me shook his head. "He's only teaching juniors." But the fact that he was hitting with John, a grown man who'd set me on course to improve my game, provided hope. Within a few weeks, I had convinced Rob to take me on as a project. Before my first lesson, I asked after his shoulder.

"Getting better," he said, reaching for it with his left hand.

"But that's your right shoulder. You're a lefty."

"What gave you that idea?"

"When I first saw you, I'm sure you were hitting with your left hand."

"Oh, that." He shrugged. "I'd just had a procedure so I had to be really careful with it for a few weeks. I was hitting with the left for a while during lessons."

This news astonished me. Rob had a stroke that most aspiring tennis players would kill for, and he'd been swinging with his opposite hand.

Later, I'd learn that Rob had been something of a local phenom. He'd played first singles for the high school team when he was just thirteen, destroying kids four or five years older. On tour, his serve approached a hundred and thirty miles an hour and he ranked in the world's top three hundred. (But he would never crack the top one hundred players. He was finished as a competitor by the time I saw him, though neither of us knew that at the time.)

We commenced the lessons, twice a week, with intensive play in between. Before I knew it, I could really hit a tennis ball. Not as the pros hit one exactly, but with more force and spin than ever before.

Most of my time with Rob, he'd put me through drills with balls fed from a hopper. But once in a while we'd rally together at my limit. At such times, of course, for the most part I would be working my tail off while Rob looked like he was standing still. Now and then, if I made him run for a good shot, he'd turn on the jets and get there with (it seemed like) hours to spare. He might hit a winner off that or play it up, keeping me in the point. If the latter, that suddenly open court on his side disappeared by the time I initiated my swing, and the rally was on again.

His game, as always, was a thing of beauty. You struggled to keep yourself from pausing just to watch the sweet purity with which he contacted the ball, the whisk from which he generated power. On rare moments when I teased him into swinging away, there was no perceptible effort added to his stroke, just a kind of increased efficiency. On those occasions, the ball spun as if it had an engine inside. It bit the court and carried itself off before I could take two steps in the right direction.

Just seeing that ball inspired me to new heights. I began going through league opponents like a power sander taking the lumps out. They couldn't handle the combination of pace and consistency, and I knew I'd made a huge leap when a guy who'd played me close the year before left the court muttering, "Too many weapons."

This was a different feeling than I'd ever had on any field of play. I stepped out on the court and went into a zone, setting my opponents back on their heels. Even when I lost a point, I was dictating play. Guys weren't merely failing to return some of my hits; they were late to the ball by a foot. One opponent showed up looking a little slow (frankly, possibly a little drunk), and my game sent him flopping to the ground twice in one hour. He left the hard court with blood dripping down his face.

Naturally, not soon after that, my game plateaued. Improvement couldn't go on much longer – not at my age, and probably not with my level of talent. My body started to hurt. The novelty of my newly acquired strokes began to wear off. Most important, Rob was preparing to move on, to chase his dream on tour one last time.

Knowing our time together would soon end, I had a hankering to see some amazing ground strokes, not to mention the rocket serve that – if I could reach it at all – would sometimes tear the racket from my hand. I began razzing him playfully, stoking the competitive spirit, and that day he gave the trash talk right back to me, challenging me to hit him the best serve I could manage. By the look in his eye, I knew how he planned to respond: with a winner that would slap the curtain behind me like a ball launched from a cannon. I reared back anyway, pivoted my hips and shoulders, and made perfect contact. I let my follow-through carry me forward, and in the next fraction of a second, I watched the ball grab the T and accelerate past Rob's outstretched racket. Ace!

We paused in mutual shock, contemplating this thing of unspeakable beauty made even more ineffable by the sheer surprise of it. For, though I'd hit the ball well and placed it perfectly, Rob's failure to lay a racket on that serve was a complete fluke. If I had ten thousand more tries ... a million ... ten million, I'd never ace a pro on his level again. A conflicted look crossed his face, pride in his student tinged with embarrassment. Then Rob challenged me to try again, but I shook my head, walked off the court, and set my racket down.

You don't top a shot as beautiful as that. You just let it linger.

Angela Tung

BLEMISHED

when I was growing up, people told me
I was dark and I believed

my own darkness
in the mirror, in my soul, my own narrow vision

— Nellie Wong, "When I Was Growing Up"

When I was growing up, I had secret freckles. They remained hidden till I removed my glasses, then I heard, "You have freckles! How cute!" by white friends.

I stopped wearing glasses and my freckles turned into splotches. Blobs.

Blemishes.

My white friends still thought they were cute. Asian women felt otherwise.

"I have the perfect whitening cream for you."

"You should really wear more makeup."

"Have you thought of a laser peel?"

Asian women were hell-bent on eradicating my darkness, as though it were their own.

WHEN I WAS GROWING UP, I WAS CONSIDERED FAT. AT MOST, I was chubby, but in my mother's eyes, I might as well have been obese.

My mother tried to "encourage" me to lose weight by saying:

"Your butt sticks out."

"You're getting a double chin."

And in front of my skinny brother and skinny friend: "Two too skinny, one too fat."

My mother always compared me to this skinny friend. She wanted me to have this friend's straight As, her outgoingness, her easy politeness with adults. My mother wanted me to be this skinny friend, to be not-me.

When I was growing up, I was always on a diet, the first when I was eight. I ate three healthy meals and fruit for snacks and dessert. I didn't eat cookies, cake, ice cream, or salty, crunchy snacks.

It was probably the smartest diet I've ever been on.

I also ran. I ran like crazy at recess and on the weekends playing running bases and tag with my friends. I ran by myself in our backyard, around and around, or else after a Frisbee I had thrown myself, catching it in midair. I ran so fast, I nearly ran over rabbits. I ran so fast, I beat the fastest kids in relay racing and on the soccer field (though I couldn't kick a ball to save my life). I surprised everyone with my speed. I ran so fast, I thought I could fly.

I ran because I wanted long skinny legs, like the girls pirouetting in *The Sound of Music*, or Daisy Duke in her daisy dukes, or like in a picture I saw once of a girl starving, her legs all bones.

I lost weight. I don't know how much, but everyone commented on it. The doctor, my friend's father who liked to throw us kids over his shoulder, even my mother.

"Doesn't it feel good to be thin?" she asked me, helping me try on smaller pants.

But my mother doesn't remember this. When I ask her, "Remember when I was little and I lost all that weight?" she shakes her head.

"You lost weight?" she asks back.

In my mother's mind, I was always fat.

WHEN I WAS GROWING UP, I TRIED TO STARVE MYSELF. I WAS NOT successful. I'd skip breakfast, which was easy, and lunch, which was hard. By the time I got home from school, I was ravenous and ate everything in sight.

When I was growing up, I escaped to my friend Linda's house every day. Linda's mother didn't yell or pick on her about her weight or take away her radio when she got Cs. At Linda's house, we could drink all the soda we wanted. Once, we ate an entire family pack of Reese's Peanut Butter Cups.

When I was growing up, I got fat going to Linda's house.

WHEN I WAS GROWING UP, I WANTED TO BE LIKE MY FRIEND Elise. Elise was a ballerina with lithe limbs, huge eyes, and a pert Irish nose. I thought if I stretched my arms farther in swimming, they'd elongate; if I reached my legs more in running, they'd grow; if I pinched my nose whenever I blew it, it'd narrow.

Of course, none of that happened.

I thought hidden behind my glasses were big double-lidded eyes, like my grandfather's, my father's father. People said I looked like father's mother, except that she was so bony, I thought I'd break her when I sat on her lap.

But when I removed my glasses, I didn't find big, double-lidded eyes. I found one eye big and one small, like my father's, even worse than two small eyes.

I tried to wear mascara, eye shadow, and liner. But none of it looked right. The mascara flaked painfully, the shadow seemed flat, the liner did nothing except run.

"Maybe you need more," my friends told me, my well-meaning, big-eyed friends.

But I didn't want to use more. I didn't want to look like the woman my parents and their friends had dubbed Panda Face because of her black-ringed eyes. I didn't want to look like Connie Chung, who despite all her makeup still looked Chinese.

WHEN I WAS GROWING UP, OUR HOUSE WAS SURROUNDED BY whiteness. White neighborhood, white school, white friends. "What are you anyway, Mexican?" boys in my nursery school would ask.

"Chink," said the kids at the bus stop. "Ching chong," whispered a boy in my high school math class.

When I was growing up, there were very few other Chinese. David who was older; Amy who was younger. One day there was a boy with an unpronounceable name full of Xs who cried every day on the bus. The driver put him near me and my brother.

"He may feel better with his own kind," she said.

He wasn't my kind. I knew English. I didn't cry till my nose filled with snot. I didn't wear weird sweaters that smelled like mothballs. I didn't stand up the whole bus ride.

"Sit," I said to him in Mandarin, and he sat.

When I was growing up, our house was Chinese. Chinese words, tastes, and smells. Chinese accents, yelling, and expectations. A Chinese grandmother who spoke no English, a Chinese grandfather who insisted on early-morning walks past our bus stop and stopped to talk to us in his broken English.

"One, two, three, four," he'd say, counting us, and laugh.

"Your grandpa can count," a boy would say, and I'd say nothing. I'd shrink and will my grandfather to disappear.

WHEN I WAS GROWING UP, I WANTED TO BE SOMEONE ELSE.

I wanted to be a movie star, part Italian, part French.

I wanted to be a singer. I wanted to dance. I wanted a strong, yet patient mother who was once a ballerina, a father who was a fellow actor, reticent yet loving. I wanted parents who supported me in everything I did.

When I was growing up, I wanted to undo my parentage. In so doing, I wanted to undo myself.

WHEN I WAS GROWING UP, I HAD CRUSHES ON ONLY WHITE BOYS. "Asian boys are like my cousins," I said. "My brothers." Only white boys came close to the movie stars I liked. Only white boys were worthy. Asian boys were lesser. Asian boys who liked me were lesser still.

When I was growing up, I didn't think a white boy would ever like me, would ever turn his head the way heads turned when Elise walked by. If a boy said he liked me, I assumed he was making fun of me, that there was something wrong with him. I assumed he wasn't special enough.

WHEN I WAS GROWING UP, I MOVED TO A NEW NEIGHBORHOOD and was no longer surrounded by whiteness. There were kids who looked like me. Kids with parents who had accents. Kids with accents themselves. I no longer felt ugly. I no longer thought about the shape of my eyes, the length of my legs.

I was no longer "the Chinese girl," but the new girl, then the angry poet girl. The girl who rarely spoke, but I didn't care.

No one called me chink or ching chong.

I went away to college and found even more people like me, people who had grown up around whiteness, who had swallowed it up. Let it swallow them whole.

I fell in love with one Asian man, then another. I fell in love with an Asian man who loved all that I hated about myself. My round face and pale skin. My freckles, sturdy legs, and dark eyes. My reticence, tomboyishness, and bookishness. He loved me for who I was.

Or so I thought.

He knew that when I was growing up, I wanted to be a writer. That I still did. Yet he chastised me for not making enough money, for not caring much about money at all.

When I was growing up, I didn't imagine caring for a sick person, for a mother not my own. My parents didn't expect us to take care of them. All we had to do was show up, bring a little something, set the table, wash the dishes. Let them know we cared.

Really, they expected so little.

My husband expected much more. Every holiday at his parents' house. Every Saturday taking care of his mother, wracked by Parkinson's disease. I held her walking from the bed, into the shower, up and down the stairs. The whole time I held her, I was afraid she'd fall. If she fell, it would be my fault—as, it seemed, everything was.

I fed her, and listened to her talk; I listened to her delusions and tried to discern what was real and what was not.

"You're such a good daughter-in-law," my friends told me. But I didn't care. I only did what I did to make my husband happy, or if not happy, then not angry. I did what I did, and I began to resent it.

I didn't expect to have to earn love.

We didn't talk about these things, my husband and I. He tried, but everything out of his mouth was a knife wound. Nothing I did was good enough, but I didn't know how to make it better. I didn't know what to do.

I LEFT OUR BED AT DAWN EVERY MORNING TO GO RUNNING. Four, five, six miles on the treadmill. Only while running did I feel accomplished, as good as, good enough.

Then suddenly I *was* good enough, in some ways. I was thin. I was beautiful. "*Ne me shou!*" my mother cried, impressed. So skinny!

I was happy she was happy. What I didn't know was that underneath, she was worried that something was wrong.

Because something was wrong, for although I was beautiful, my husband no longer wanted me. He seemed to no longer want anything. All he saw was darkness. All he knew was rage. Everyone was against him. All was going to end, no matter what he did, so he might as well end it himself.

Although I was beautiful, my husband went with another. Although I was his wife, he gave another his child. Although he still loved me (so he said), he betrayed me in the worst possible way.

And yet I couldn't leave. Because he still loved me, because he was all I had known. Because he was the first who made me feel beautiful.

I ran. I ran to forget, to not feel, to hear only breathing, my own heart, the rhythm of my feet. I ran and ran, trying to escape the darkness. But I could not. When I stopped running, the darkness was still there.

WHEN I WAS GROWING UP, I WANTED TO BE BEAUTIFUL.

If I were beautiful, I'd be approved of, applauded, loved.

I became beautiful, and it made no difference.

I know there's more to being beautiful. I want to believe.

I want to believe that these white hairs on my head don't need dyeing.

That these new wrinkles are perfectly natural.

I want to believe that my freckles aren't splotches, blobs, or blemishes. That anyone who tells me otherwise is seeing only their own darkness, that it's their own darkness they're afraid of, that it might swallow them whole.

I want to believe my new love will love me, no matter what. Even as I gain unsightly bulges, retreat into my old shyness, and battle, still, the same darkness from all those years ago, he will continue to love me as he does now.

I want to believe that, like the other, he loves those things about me that I hate, but also more. That he wants me to flourish, to be me but better. To be less afraid, to see that my fears hurt more than myself. To believe that it's who I am and not what I do that he loves.

I want to believe it. I almost do.

But I am still growing up.

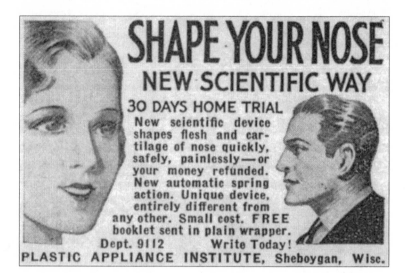

JESSICA ANYA BLAU

SEE YA LATER, BIG NOSE

1. IT STARTED IN FIFTH GRADE WITH PAUL B. HE REMINDED ME of both Charlie Brown and the father on *Eight Is Enough*—a perfectly circular head, blond velvet-fuzzy hair, pale blue eyes. I wouldn't say I had a crush on him, but I definitely watched him. His yard was long and fenced and mysterious. He darted around, never walking on a single side of any street.

"Jessica would be cute if she didn't have such a big nose," he told ... I don't know; it seemed like he told *everyone*. It came back to me several times. From Kenny J., who was skinny and funny and had sent me love notes in third grade. And from Karen S., who always seemed older than everyone and knew what people were doing and saying at all times the way a mother might. And from Rena B., who lived on the end of my cul-de-sac and was movie-star beautiful but thought she looked like a troll (she sort of did, but she was still impossibly gorgeous).

Following Paul B.'s report, I spent hours in the bathroom staring at my nose and wondering if I'd be cute if it weren't so big. I examined my nose from every angle: straight on, up, down, profile. When I pulled the mirrored medicine cabinet door open I was able to see my profile reflected from the wall mirror above the sink. This was probably the most examined pose. I knew, and still know, the differences between my left and right profiles. (Sometime in high school I came up with the theory that if I lived in the UK where the car wheel is on the right side, I'd never have dated as much as I did. My left profile, I've always believed, is far superior to my right and this fact, I honestly thought, kept those driving boys interested in me as I sat to their right.)

2. SIXTH GRADE: MY NEW BEST FRIEND JULIE T. WAS OBSESSED with the movie and soundtrack to *Funny Girl*. She played the record every day after school and sang along while staring at Barbra Streisand's glowing face on the album cover.

"You look just like her!" Julie always said. "*Exactly.*" I didn't get it. One day I forced the issue.

"*How* do I look like her?" I asked.

"Your nose," Julie said, "you have the same nose." Did we? I didn't think we did. I still don't think we do; her nostrils are more pronounced than mine. But I remembered my mother talking about Barbra. "Everyone respects her," my mother had said, "because she didn't get a nose job." Was my nose like that? Was my nose so big that the choice *not* to get a nose job would seem respectable and brave? It sounded like deciding not to wear false teeth, or letting your foggy-blue, runny, blind eye be seen instead of putting on sunglasses, or wearing a bikini on a California beach when you're a hundred and fifty pounds overweight because G-D-it, you're just as entitled to a good swim as the thin people!

3. SOMETIME AFTER COLLEGE, WHEN I WAS STILL LIVING IN THE Bay Area, I was driving through Oakland on a beautiful day when sunlight was flooding everything into a golden white. All my windows were down and the wind was blowing my hair across my face. I stopped at a long red light on a quiet street. There was a gorgeous black man in a red convertible next to me. Everything about him was sexy: his ropey, muscled arm extended to the steering wheel, his smooth, clear skin, his square, white teeth. I looked at him. He looked at me. I smiled. He smiled. I looked some more. He looked some more. I hoped he'd ask me for my number, or pull over so we could chat, or maybe he'd even follow me until I stopped. And then the light changed. I paused before hitting the gas. He turned his head toward me and said, "See ya later, Big Nose!" I drove slowly and let him spin out of sight.

4. FOR YEARS NOW, I HAVE CONFISCATED PHOTOS OF MYSELF that were taken in profile (always without my consent as I have been turning *toward* the camera since Paul B.'s first comment) and coloring in the bump in my nose with a Sharpie to see what I'd look like with a smaller nose (I look like someone who isn't me). I've shown these doctored photos to other people, who often stare at me as if I'm presenting them a picture of toe fungus. They claim not to get what I'm speaking of when I speak of my big nose. I imagine they're all trying to be polite.

5. NOT LONG AGO I WAS AT THE SEWANEE WRITERS' CONFERENCE in Tennessee. I walked into the dining room alone one night, saw an empty chair next to a nice-looking older man, and sat down. He was charming, funny; we laughed uproariously throughout the meal. At some point, I realized he was also famous. Famous in that way of someone *People* magazine would never recognize but any graduate student in America would. A couple of people approached him to sign books. Others were watching him.

After dinner, we walked together down the road to another building where there was going to be a reading. Our conversation from the dinner table had continued. In the middle of this, in the middle of a sentence, he stopped, put his hand on my forearm, and said, "My god! I hadn't seen what a big, beautiful nose you have!"

"You think my nose is big?" I asked.

"It wasn't apparent when we were looking straight at each other at the table, but here it is!"

"Here *my big nose* is?"

"Yes! And it's beautiful!" He seemed genuinely excited, as if he'd found enormous bouncy breasts under a sweatshirt, or tumbling hair beneath a baseball cap. I vowed right then to buy every single one of his books even if I had no intention of ever reading them.

6. IF YOU WATCHED THE SHOW *SIX FEET UNDER*, YOU KNOW THAT every episode started with a death. They were wonderful deaths, sometimes funny, not always sad, usually fascinating. In one episode, a group of middle-aged women are getting ready to walk into something, maybe a movie or a concert. One of them gets a nosebleed. She sends her friends in ahead of her and stands on the sidewalk

trying to abate the flow. And then she collapses. In the next scene, we learn that she had died from a massive blood clot due to a long-ago nose job. The fact that one can later die from a nose job was a thrilling discovery for me—forget being brave like Barbra, or bold like obese people who wear bikinis on the beach; I was saving my own life by living with this nose!

7. THERE ARE VERY FEW BIG NOSE ROLE MODELS IN THE WORLD. There's Sarah Jessica Parker (I've been told many times that I remind people of her but have never pushed the issue enough to find out if it's the nose), Sofia Coppola (I was thrilled when she was in the Marc Jacobs ads), and . . . who? Name one. Find one. The list dwindles each year. Ashlee Simpson had what the famous writer would call a "big, beautiful nose!" and had it fixed. Ditto Jennifer Grey. Even Cameron Diaz, Gisele Bündchen, Megan Fox, and Jennifer Aniston, who weren't even Big Nose Role Models, had what little they were born with reduced.

8. THIS ESSAY WOULD BE MUCH MORE APPEALING, CORRECT IN the feminist landscape, and mature, even, if I told you that I have accepted my nose, I love my nose, I worship The Nose! Instead, sadly, I must tell you my recurring fantasy: I'm hit by a car, or I'm in a building that explodes, or maybe I'm in a plane crash, and my nose is smashed. *It is essential that I get a nose job!* Also, the fat on my arms and thighs has somehow been blown away (the stitches leave no scars!) and my split ends are burned off. It's all terrifying! Horrifying! Dramatic! But in the end, I look cute enough for the likes of Paul B.

97

QUENBY MOONE

THE QUIET LIGHT

SAT BY MY FATHER'S BED. IF THERE WAS ONE PLACE IN THE
house I was often sitting, it was there, next to him. Holding his
hand, reading to him, listening to him reminisce about how still,
after all these years, he hated his mother, or that he loved his grand-
mother, or that the light was fading.

This was sometimes metaphoric; Dad's light was fading, the last
embers cooling, as were his hands, his circulation now committed to
keeping what remained of his vital organs ticking, with the conse-
quence of deathly cold fingers and feet. Even the tip of his nose was
cold, although that might be a feature of our family, since my nose
is often cold, as well. I don't read much into it, anyway.

Sometimes the fading light was literal, my father lying in his
living room, waiting for his last hours to unwind with the ebbs and
flows of day turning to night and back again. There was little else
that changed there from his vantage point; stillness enveloped our
days, punctuated by visits by hospice workers, or strange mortality-
driven crises, and then back again into the tides of changing light.

This light might not be enough for some people. This light might be too slow in its ascents and descents: The coolness of morning summer dawn, shedding blue ripples through the curtains before spectrum changes of orange and pink, arcing up through the trees and over flowers, creeping along the vinca and lavender, sprays of crocosmia, touching spots of dusty earth and moving into the cracks of sidewalks, tipping farther north in the sky. Tinting and warming where it falls, the windows through which my father gazed, where my father lay, looking out into his garden with eyes that could no longer see.

But the light was enough for him.

My father, as the artist Charles Moone, spent his life looking at light as it fell across the water, as it trickled through the trees, as it revealed mysteries of skin on top of fabric in a life-drawing class, exposing the knob of an ankle or hiding the shape of an eye under a brow; this was Dad's natural realm, and he was quite at home with the slow changes of light, including his own.

IF ONE HAS NEVER BEEN A WITNESS TO DEATH AND DYING, LIKE I hadn't, it seems we do nothing but fear its aspect. How do people die? Is it grisly? Gruesome? Painful? Is it slow, fast, horrible? Shocking and surprising? Eerily mundane?

It is all these things. What I hadn't counted on was its beauty.

THERE WERE SO MANY THINGS I DIDN'T KNOW WHEN MY FATHER was given word that his time was up. We had worked through his cancer diagnosis for a year, but it was a zero-sum game: The cancer was bigger than any medical intervention.

I knew that hospice was something people had as they died; what it was or what took place during hospice care was completely mysterious. So when I was given the names of agencies to call, I didn't know what was on offer.

It turns out that hospice is a lot more, and a lot less, than I imagined. Their involvement was imperative but, in the big scheme, limited. Two nurse visits a week, unless there was an emergency. On-call access to medical care twenty-four hours a day; they even dropped off nausea medication at 1 A.M. when my father couldn't take his morphine because of a crummy tummy.

A physical therapist arrived to show my brother and me how to move Dad around in bed without throwing a disk; she came once a week to help us learn how to wrap a belt around Dad and plunk him on the loo, until it became clear that he would actually never leave bed again. And his personal aide, Ric, was perhaps the most important piece of the hospice puzzle and possibly the least romantic: Ric came twice a week to bathe Dad, swaddle him in new sheets, buff him up, trim his nails, comb his hair—what was left, anyway. Ric was, for us, a cheerleader when my brother and I were completely at sea; he told us raunchy jokes (presumably not usually a part of hospice service but imperative in our case) and encouraged us to believe that we were doing the right things at the right times. Ric was heroic to our very small universe.

But that was it: A total of four or five guaranteed visits a week from hospice workers. Emergencies were of course attended to, but if there was no emergency, then no visit. My brother and I were Dad's only caregivers.

This left us with a lot of time.

DAD LOOKED THROUGH HIS WINDOWS IN HIS LAST DAYS WITH eyes trained to see by years of teaching others how to see. An art historian and professor for over thirty years, his vision was tempered by light, could see the absence of it. Objects are meaningless without both, and so he saw both with clarity. Light and shadow were tangible to Dad, things that created shape out of nothingness.

At the end of his life, Dad's eyesight became dim. His sight began to retreat into uselessness just like his circulation. But because he was trained to see light, when light was the only thing that remained, it still moved him. He traced lines in his sheets, which had become blurry, but his mind, still sharp despite all that befell him, created paintings with what light was left. He traced pictures there, like a child creating elephants out of clouds. "I see you there," he said one day. I couldn't; it was for him only.

My father watched from his window as the light tipped south; Dad was bedridden from mid-July, and by August, as his light was dipping, the light outside was sinking, as well. He noted this. He wanted to make it through the summer and the warmth of direct sun, but not longer. He didn't want to be without light in the cold, long dark of Portland winter.

His eyes, with rings around them, still twinkled with impish delight at jokes we would tell. In midsummer, the sun was too far north to cross onto his bed by the window, but by August it began to creep forth across his sheets, splitting his body into islands of light and dark. The light fell over divots in his skin, his shin bones, his sheets.

His glasses, thick, ponderous, cumbersome, were now useless to Dad and so they were abandoned to his bedside table. I hadn't seen my father without his glasses since I was a child; his face came forward, broke through the illness and suffering. I found the younger man from other days: strong cheekbones, arched brow, devilish smile. His beard, stark white, growing fuller with neither of his helpers (my brother and I) clever enough to master the task of trimming it, made him regal in aspect, a goodly King Charles lying in his chamber waiting for his end in peaceful repose.

My father's hazel eyes turned cerulean, like the eyes of newborns; I thought I was making it up, that maybe his eyes had always been blue and I had made a mistake. His eyes became fog-enshrouded wells that saw only the light and hints of shape but no form. My mother asked, "Did his eyes turn blue?" and I was relieved. I couldn't believe I would have made up a basic fact like that. My father's eyes turned as blue as the ocean, shades of twilight.

I SAT BY MY FATHER'S BED, SHADOWS AND LIGHT FILLING IN the hours through which we waited for his end. And when it came, the light was blue, day only hinted at in the barest needle of light peeking through his thin linen curtains, the outlines of trees and plants mere suggestions to be filled in at some other hour. The stillness of the hour and the light was one in which Dad was quite at home, painting them in deep purples and blues, echoed in dawns and dusks, the bookends to each day, hinting at wonder without revealing too much.

In these quiet hours, in this quiet light, Dad was at home.

STEVE SPARSHOTT

FIN

ELLO. WELCOME TO THE GENTS.

The men's room, restroom, bathroom, as we don't call it. The toilet, loo, lavatory, bog, pisser, or trap, as we do. "We" are British.

The Gents – this word is never apostrophised, for some reason.

It doesn't smell good in the gents. As any woman who's ever ventured in there will tell you, "It *stinks!*"

Well, yes, it does. In the gents, body-temperature urine is sprayed onto a cold ceramic or metal surface, and then it evaporates, filling the air (and, consequently, your lungs) with microscopic piss particles. As the night progresses, the streams in the men's room become more forceful, more expansive, and less accurate.

Oh dear, you might be thinking. A British male talking about public lavatories; this must be yet another tale of a misunderstood homosexual aesthete plying his trade in the gents lav under Hyde Park Corner. I don't actually know if there is, or has ever been, a public toilet under Hyde Park Corner, although there's an underground car park there, which I'm sure is in regular use as a *pissoir.* If an indoor car park were to be built in the shape of a race-track, or completely circular, in the absence of corners would men still mark their territory? On a Friday night, would there be drunk blokes running round and round, trying to find somewhere to relieve themselves?

Traditionally, Hampstead Heath's the place to go for a bit of no-strings, boy-on-boy action. "Cottaging," it's also called. Toilet trading.

Just as every graphic designer is expected to have a favourite font, product designers are sometimes asked to name small, everyday objects that excite them. Paperclips are popular. You know key rings, or, rather, the steel loop that coils round on itself twice, the bit you wriggle and slide the keys onto? Those are good, too, and the design is actually unregistered; nobody knows who invented them. The simplest, most functional items have the most fans; my favourite's the ball clasp or kiss lock: the beautifully simple latch mechanism on a purse, in which two brass balls slide round each other. I don't want to sound like Insane Clown Posse, but when you think about it, zips are pretty amazing, too.

It really doesn't smell good in the gents. Whether they're elegant expanses of heavy white porcelain or prison-aesthetic folded steel, communal urinals are the worst offenders. Late in the evening, near last orders, a solo user will indulge himself, spraying the entire width or chasing the brightly colored freshener tablets along the trench.

Individual pods are slightly less odorous, and not such a social challenge. Not as much fun, true; the single bowl encourages more precise aim, as each user has his own clear target (the drain), set centrally within white space, his own personal white space, delineated by porcelain fins protruding from the wall.

These fins, these urinal dividers: You probably wouldn't notice as you're suffocating in the stench, but they're incredibly elegant, simple, sculptural things.

Unless they're intended to act like blinders, reducing your peripheral vision to *THX1138* blank whiteness, dividers are not for privacy. It's far too easy to look over at the next chap's chap (if you're so inclined) or for him to look at yours (if he's so inclined). Ideally, neither, or both, but they're probably there as splash guards, protecting everyone from their neighbors' gusto.

My admiration of urinal dividers goes against the function-over-form principles of my industrial design background. My absolute top choice for aesthetics is the shark fin shape. What do they do? Not much. *Maybe* they prevent strangers from urinating on us; *maybe* they perform a psychological function; *maybe* they keep us in line (both physically and behaviourally) – but not really. They're a bit useless and pointless, and therein lies their appeal; an attempt to create something with a prosaic, base function has resulted in a piece of pure, uncluttered form.

I'd like to own one. A new, clean, fin-shaped urinal divider, straight from the manufacturer – not one with, um, narrative. I'd put it in the middle of my kitchen table, as if a white porcelain shark were swimming just below the surface. Men would work out what it was after a while, although seeing it out of context – literally off the wall – might throw them at first. Women? Maybe. Eventually.

I'd explain to everybody that it was factory fresh. And then we could all have a nice cup of tea.

LANCE REYNALD

BLACK PAINT

… how did I get here?

4 A.M. THE COLD PURITY OF NIGHT SNOW IS FALLING GEN-
tly outside the windows. My mind wanders to an October sky
along the coast, scarcely more than a year ago. My memory jogged
by a snapshot on the table in front of me. I woke suddenly and had
to rummage through my desk drawer to find the photograph.

"Baby, what you doing here?"

Even though his words are sleepy soft, he has broken the silence
I've been trying to understand for the past hour and a half. I hear
him, but the words aren't reaching me. My mind has been grabbing
at memories and song lyrics trying to figure out how it is that I've
come to be here now. The Talking Heads are playing a prophetic
loop.

… and you may find yourself in another part of the world.

I AM, BUT NEVER WOULD HAVE BEEN IF NOT FOR THE TWO
years with her that preceded coming here. The snapshot of her face
with her usually immaculate bob windswept as we walked along
the deserted, off-season beach. In the middle of our argument, I
snapped the photo with the camera she'd bought me at the Sun-
day flea market shortly after we moved in together. I had shown her
some of the contact sheets of the photos I'd taken in school. She had
said the shots were beautiful, that I had what they called an eye for
it. She wanted to know why I wasn't still taking pictures. I told her
that I'd given it up. I didn't think it was something that would ever
lead to anything, or more accurately, that my father didn't think it
was going to lead to anything. I'd lost my camera from back in my
school days and hadn't thought to replace it since it had been just a
passing hobby that couldn't lead to anything.

"Being able to see beauty is a gift. It doesn't have to lead to
anything but that." She wasn't challenging anything, just stating a
belief. She put the neck strap over my head as she placed the camera
in my hands and said, "It's time you start seeing again."

… and you may find yourself in a beautiful house, with a beautiful wife.

THE APARTMENT WE SHARED WAS OUR BEAUTIFUL HOUSE,
though she wasn't a wife. I'd asked after a few months and she'd
refused. Not because of the fact that she was twenty years older than
me, but because "wife" wasn't a thing she'd ever wanted to be, and
I shouldn't believe that my happiness could be so simply answered,

either. We could be lovers for a while; that was permitted. She could teach me to see the world around me again and we'd remain friends, no matter what. She had plans for us and great hopes for me while the traditional rules of society were of no importance to her, us.

I started to see again. The spent canisters of film dropped into the candy dish on the table in the entry hall of our apartment, replaced by a fresh roll of black-and-white film from the top shelf of the refrigerator door. The contact sheets from the lab were always on the kitchen table with the magnifying glass nearby. Together, we'd look through the images of our world as I had seen and documented it and find the perfect ones to enlarge. She then sent them to the frame shop to be matted and framed so she could become curator of the exhibit on our dining room walls.

Even away from the lens, I was seeing beauty again. Leaning against the door frame of our bedroom, watching her at her dressing table using a toothbrush to scoop black dye from a bowl and touch up her graying roots between visits to the salon. Silently sitting there with her eyes closed waiting the thirty-five minutes it took for the color to erase the years between us. Watching from across the table at the bistro as she raised the glass of red wine to her lips, the deep burgundy gently staining the scarlet cream of lipstick before a gentle smile at the berry tones of the vintage passed across her face.

To help sharpen my sight, she painted the walls of our apartment a flat black and the furnishings were a study of textures in black from satin to gloss. She said the effect would help me sense the details of everything else. Dinner guests became more vivid and animated. A solitary bright silk scarf printed with equestrian buckles draped on a hook by the front door. The graceful white ribbons of smoke from her Dunhill cigarette pulled from the distinctive blue box would drift toward the ceiling, lingering against the dark backdrop. The box of chocolate croissants fresh from the bakery atop the dining table appeared as a shock of bright color, and my nose filled with the bold aroma of espresso brewed in the double-chambered Italian pot over the gas flame of the stove. Every detail sensed, even beyond sight.

In that first year, I became conscious of the art that was our life together, and her dining room exhibition of my photographs began to spill into the other rooms of our apartment as I created more images to share with her the details that my eyes noted in our first year together. The more pictures I took, the more refined my vision became, the products of her encouragement and direction.

It was during our second year together that she started selecting the best images and gathering them in a portfolio. Tirelessly, she visited her friends in the galleries and showed them my work, determined to get me a showing. She thought it was time for others to see our world through my eyes. After months of campaigning on her part, we were asked to submit eight photographs for a group show. Together, we looked through thousands of frames on the contact sheets and selected the eight that she would deliver to the gallery in a taxi.

It was a Thursday night in the August heat, and I stood nervously in the corner of the gallery and held tightly to a plastic cup of cheap white wine as she stood by my side and proudly discussed my photographs with the gallery patrons. For me, the work was something we shared; it was our life together and a way of seeing she had cultivated in me. To have her do all the talking for me was the most natural thing in the world. She found the perfect words for the conversation I could only show in pictures. My sight was the product of our collaboration. I felt as though my feet were nailed to the floor as she talked for hours and the crowd dwindled to just a few.

In the last moments of my first gallery exhibition, she started a conversation with a Frenchman in a shabby gray suit. He was another photographer, whose work hung on the wall opposite my own. Together, they crossed the room to look at his images as I stood against my wall and watched them.

While my work was a study of the objects in our world, his were portraits of the people he'd encountered that summer, strong images that captured the beauty of the ordinary people passed in his travels. His photos had a voice of photojournalism compared to the fine art captured by my lens. As she studied each image intently, he told her the stories of the people he had photographed. When they finally returned to my side of the room, she introduced the two of us, and we shook hands. His grip was strong and his gaze direct; my eyes darted between the two of them, unsure of what I should say or do next.

She excused herself to the ladies' room and left us standing in front of my photographs. Finally, the Frenchman pointed to one of my images and asked me about it. I tried my best to remember how I had heard her describe the contrast and composition to another person earlier in the evening and repeat it.

"It is not so easy for you to put in words?" His direct gaze was followed by a smile.

"No, I don't like talking much."

"Easier to show, yes?"

As I shoved my free hand into my pants pocket, I raised the plastic cup and finished the last gulp of wine with a nod: *Yes.*

After the opening, the Frenchman started to spend more time with us. She thought it would be good for us to become friends; he could help me take my art to someplace new. He joined us for dinners at home that would last into the early hours of morning, the three of us on the sofa, drinking bottle after bottle of red wine as we talked.

For entertainment, we would venture out to a jazz club a few blocks from our apartment. The two of them would talk and laugh for hours in French, and I often couldn't keep up with the speed of their conversations, able to understand only a few words here and there. I wasn't jealous, but I was uncertain of her interest in him. The beautiful world we had shared as two had become a new world of three. Something had changed, but I couldn't quite figure it out.

And you may ask yourself, well ... how did I get here?

THE THREE OF US TOOK AN OFF-SEASON TRIP TO THE COAST. IT was October, and most things there had been boarded up for the coming winter. He slept in at the rented bungalow as she and I took our morning walks along the beach. My uncertainty had started to fade, and I accepted the Frenchman as one of us.

On the morning of our last walk along the beach, she and I argued. He was moving back to France in a week, and she thought I should join him there. She said he still had things to teach me that would make my work great; I would be a fool not to go. She said that he could teach me to see people the way she had taught me to see things.

"But I do see people."

"No, you don't. You're missing what's right in front of you."

She had made up her mind that I would be moving away. She had also made sure it would be with someone who would protect and care for me as she had. I didn't understand it that day, but I knew I had to go because it was what she wanted for me.

The snapshot in my hands reminds me of the argument. An October sky with the light softened by the early-morning autumn haze. The wind whipping her immaculate coiffure against her cheeks as she tries to push it back behind her ear with the delicate arch of her fingers. The photograph as proof that even in an argument, I was able to see her in a moment of beauty, as she lived every moment, right in front of me.

GINA FRANGELLO

WHAT
YOU
SEE

An Intelligent Woman and a Beautiful Woman go on vacation together with their Husbands. They go on a cruise, to Greece. The Intelligent Woman worries that her husband will like the Beautiful Woman's breasts when they take off their bathing suit tops on the beach. Yet to refuse to remove her own top in hopes of forcing the Beautiful Woman to remain clothed in solidarity, the Intelligent Woman would have to be willing to portray herself as Conservative, Modest, and Unworldly. Someone who does not understand that in Greece breasts are No Big Deal. She is uncertain what to do.

Reprinted with permission from the short story collection *Slut Lullabies,* by Gina Frangello (Emergency Press, 2010).

But wait. Is it important to know that the Intelligent Woman's Husband is more attractive (and also more successful) than the Beautiful Woman's Husband? I think it is. You see, without that knowledge you might assume (rightly, you'd think) that the Intelligent Woman has grounds to be threatened by the Beautiful Woman. You might reckon that Beautiful People have better lives. Don't they? Well, sometimes they do. But in this case, the Intelligent Woman has the Husband that all the Friends she and the Beautiful Woman share agree is the better of the two Husbands. Incidentally, all the Friends prefer the Intelligent Woman to the Beautiful Woman, too. Maybe they are jealous of the Beautiful Woman. But, to the Intelligent Woman, each other, and themselves, they simply claim to find the Beautiful Woman "nice but boring."

The Intelligent Woman and the Beautiful Woman have been on vacation together before. They have been Friends for a long time (they are now thirty-one), and when they were eighteen, they went together to Ft. Lauderdale on spring break. Afterward, they did not speak for nearly a year. Then the Beautiful Woman's Boyfriend broke up with her, and the Beautiful Woman was rumored to be suicidal. She had been witnessed causing a scene at the top of Bascom Hill on the way to class. The Beautiful Woman ripped the Boyfriend's shirt while screaming. What she screamed had something to do with the Boyfriend thinking the Models in *Vogue* were prettier than the Beautiful Woman. The Intelligent Woman did not particularly desire to renew her friendship with the Beautiful Woman (they had never been *that* close), but to refuse would have seemed heartless, given what the Beautiful Woman was going through, and as the Beautiful Woman was now considered Unstable. So the friendship was renewed.

The Intelligent Woman's Husband is, of course, an Intelligent Man. They are, in fact, Academics, which verifies their intelligence to the world, along with raising all kinds of assumptions about their sex life, some of which are true and some of which are not. One might assume, for example, that they have very cerebral sex, which is not the case. One might assume their lovemaking to be on the prudish side—also untrue. In the ten years they've been together, their sex has consisted prominently of the Intelligent Man tying up and spanking the Intelligent Woman, and the Intelligent Woman giving her Husband head. For variation, anal penetration occurs and there are escapades outdoors, in cars, and in the bathrooms of parties. Once, when abstaining from intercourse for a month before their wedding, the Intelligent Woman and the Intelligent Man hurled pornographic threats at one another for an hour while masturbating each other on the Best Man's sofa. The year following the wedding, they fucked a minimum of five times a week.

The Beautiful Woman's Husband is a Macho Man. The cruise was his idea. For all the reasons you might assume—yes, you would be right about all of that.

In Ft. Lauderdale, the Intelligent Woman and the Beautiful Woman had another traveling companion, the Aggressive Woman. On their very first night at the neon-signed bars, which the Intelligent Woman found embarrassingly contrary to the Bohemian image she wanted to project (though there was, as of yet, nobody to appreciate this projection, so the minimal lure of cheesy bars won out), the Aggressive Woman met a man. A boy, really, they were all only eighteen. He and the Aggressive Woman made out on the dance floor to a song that went: *Boom Boom Boom, Let's Go Back to My Room.* Afterward, he walked the Aggressive Woman to the hotel, where she did not invite him to her room because she, the Beautiful Woman, and the Intelligent Woman were sharing quarters. That, and because she was a Virgin, though this was as embarrassing to her as attendance at cheesy bars was to the Intelligent Woman, and so she used her roommates (really straight girls who need their sleep), not virginity, as an excuse.

The Aggressive Woman may also be referred to as: the Smoking Woman, the Skinny Woman, the Foul-Mouthed Skank, the Special-Education Teacher, the Adopted Daughter, the World Traveler, and the Survivor of Childhood Hodgkin's Disease.

On the cruise, the Beautiful Woman doubles her dose of Levsinex. The motion of the boat and all the exotic food is certain to make her Irritable Bowel Syndrome act up, which will annoy the Macho Man, who believes her illness is all in her mind and takes the opportunity of her diarrhea exoduses to mock her to any friends remaining around the dinner table, revealing her various unfounded anxieties while imitating her excitable voice until everyone howls even louder than she does when home sick on the toilet alone.

On the cruise, the Intelligent Woman brings with her Vicodin, Flexiril, and Valium. The Vicodin and Flexiril are for her bladder, which has an ulcer or something like an ulcer that is called Interstitial Cystitis and means her immune system is flawed but nobody knows how. There is no cure. The disease is neither progressive nor terminal. Men rarely get it. Doctors say the condition can be managed through rigorous avoidance of alcohol, all tomato and other citrus products, fermented foods (soy sauce, cheese), and molds (mushrooms, cheese again – she has to avoid cheese twice, though even with her limited math, 2 × 0 still equals zero). The Intelligent Woman adheres to these rules like a nun, yet her symptoms include urinating as frequently as the pregnant and a burning mock-bladder-infection twenty-four hours a day every day with no end in sight.

You might assume that the Valium is self-explanatory given the Intelligent Woman's predicament. It's not: She is afraid of planes.

The Boyfriend of the Beautiful Woman, unaware that he would break up with her in less than a year, sent her roses every day she was in Ft. Lauderdale. At the time, he thought her more beautiful than any of the Models in *Vogue*. At the time, he was terrified of nothing more than that, no matter where she went, every man would want her, and the burden of being so desired would prove too much, just as it had when the Boyfriend had relentlessly pursued and stolen her from Boyfriend Number One who had preceded him. So, every day, he sent roses to the hotel room the Beautiful Woman shared with her two Boyfriend-less Friends. But in his own cheater's heart, he knew that she would stray.

On the cruise, the Intelligent Man and the Macho Man play chess all day. The Intelligent Man wins every game.

The Intelligent Woman was once a Neighborhood Girl. She wore a jacket with her Italian surname printed on the back and encircled with red and green stars. She smoked Newport cigarettes and piled purple eye shadow up to her dark, heavy brows. Still, none of the Neighborhood Boys wanted to fuck her, because she read too much and said things that made them feel stupid, plus she sounded like an ABC Afterschool Special, going off on preachy riffs about how doing drugs instead of going to school was wrong. She even made fun of the cool words they made up (to the tone of the Pledge of Allegiance) swearing loyalty to the Neighborhood Street Gang.

The Girls on the Corner counseled the Intelligent Neighborhood Girl that she never got a guy because she was fat, so when she was thirteen she became Anorexic and lost thirty pounds quick as that, and – though her hungry breasts immediately and forever ceased all development, remaining forever pubescent – all the Neighborhood Fat Ladies said how much better she looked and how envious they were (they were Uneducated People who did not know what Anorexia was). But the Neighborhood Boys still hated her.

Then they gang-raped another Neighborhood Fat Girl, which went to show that not wanting to fuck the Intelligent Neighborhood Girl had never had anything to do with the width of her ass in the first place.

Imagine that.

On the cruise the Intelligent Woman wanders the ship library and complains that the novels are too mainstream, and then finds one she can tolerate and reads.

The Beautiful Woman does not read. Somehow she made straight As through high school and college, a feat that required copious amounts of reading. But now that there is nothing she is required to memorize for a test she does not read anymore, and she never will, but you already knew that.

When the Aggressive Woman's Ft. Lauderdale Fling told the Beautiful Woman he had fallen in love with her (in the span of three days), the Beautiful Woman let him kiss her even though he was short and stocky and a Guido who spoke with a New Jersey accent she would recall a decade later when watching *The Sopranos* on HBO. Nobody could fathom why a Beautiful Woman with a Boyfriend who sent roses every day would possibly kiss such a little toad, especially when her Best Friend, the Aggressive Woman, was so smitten with him, seeing as she preferred Guidos, for reasons of her own.

The Intelligent Woman and her Friends think, in retrospect, that they understand the Beautiful Woman's motives now. But probably they are wrong. Probably they still don't.

On the cruise, the Intelligent Man and the Macho Man play another round of chess. They speak about their Careers, though their work is not similar and they do not understand what the other does.

The Intelligent Man is an almost-renowned Scientist. The Macho Man is Regional Manager for a Best Buy and has a Company Car. But he is a good sport about losing at chess. And, being a Manager, he is a good listener, or good at pretending he is.

The Intelligent Woman failed both physics and trigonometry in high school because she was busy reading Anaïs Nin and scribbling secret poetry that did not turn out to be Any Good. She does not play chess. When her Husband discusses work too often, she cites his Presbyterian upbringing as though this is self-explanatory and necessarily a flaw.

Whenever the Beautiful Woman takes off her shirt at home, her Husband shouts, Boobies! No matter what else he is doing.

The Beautiful Woman grew up in the suburbs.
Duh!

The suburb in question is in Minnesota, and mostly Anglo-blond. The Beautiful Woman is Jewish and olive-skinned. In high school, she was not considered a Beautiful Woman. She was considered a Stingy Jew. Or a Puerto Rican, because she was so dark. That is what Boyfriend Number One was: Puerto Rican. When they were together, Minnesotans said, Look at the two Wetbacks. The Beautiful Woman loved Boyfriend Number One so fiercely, she wept every time they made love and kept his photo in her bathroom no matter how hysterical it drove her mother. He was the only one who understood.

When she got to college, she dumped him immediately for the first persistent Jew.

The Beautiful Woman told the Aggressive Woman that the kiss didn't mean anything; she was only being polite. She said the Ft. Lauderdale Fling was ugly and the Aggressive Woman could have him, although of course he didn't want her. The Aggressive Woman said, Your beak-nosed Boyfriend is ugly, too! The Beautiful Woman said, Well, I don't see anybody sending you roses, so you really have no right to judge.

The Intelligent Woman thought all the men in question were so undesirable it was literally amazing, but she didn't open her mouth because not only was she receiving no roses, she didn't even have a Fling to lose to another woman to begin with. So she kept quiet and flicked ants off the bed in their cheap room.

The Beautiful Woman daydreams about a man who looks deep into her eyes and says her name tenderly while making love. She likes kisses that are not too wet and sloppy. Whenever a man tells her she is pretty, she melts.

The Intelligent Woman has recurrent nightmares of damp, flabby sex with her mother.

Both of the Husbands, asleep and awake, dream about head.

On the cruise, which lasts for five nights, both Couples make love exactly twice, on the same days, at the same times. These are the only times they are not all together.

Afterward, the women tell each other about it in the bathroom and marvel at the coincidence.

Whenever her mouth is not otherwise engaged, the Macho Man likes the Beautiful Woman to talk dirty to him and tell him her fantasies. Though the Macho Man may not think she is smart, she is smart enough to know that he doesn't want to hear: You look into my eyes and tell me how pretty I am and how special and how much you love me and only me and would die without me in your arms. So she says other things, but often he tells her she is repetitive and unimaginative and unconvincing.

And if you think that only fuels the fire of her *actual* fantasy and makes her want to run like hell but instead she goes into the bathroom to shit with bowel-churning anxiety because she knows she never will, well. You would be right.

Both women have TMJ and dentists who pretend not to understand why their jaws never improve. And that is enough of that.

On the beach in Rhodes, the first beach they've been on, about two-thirds of the women actually have on bikini tops, or even one-piece suits. The Intelligent Woman becomes flummoxed. Life is always exceedingly more difficult when choice is involved.

That Fat Neighborhood Girl who was once raped by the Gang Boys (who are now in prison, junkies, piddly runners for the mob, or else ordinary Family Men living in the Old Neighborhood or cheap Chicago suburbs) is now a Fat Counselor. After the rape, during which she was also beaten with a coat hanger and thrown down a flight of stairs, many ladies in the neighborhood came forward to offer alibis for the Gang Rapists. One of the Rapists was the Fat Neighborhood Girl's Boyfriend, and one was a thirty-two-year-old small-time Mafioso who was president of the local school board. The Fat Neighborhood Girl and her Single Mother moved out of the Old Neighborhood down to the South Side, where other Italian people lived but where nobody knew them enough to know they were both Sluts. After they were gone, the Fat Neighborhood Ladies said, She's always been a whore, that mother, and now the daughter is, too, see what you get?

On the South Side, the Fat Neighborhood Girl did not have any more Boyfriends and developed a fascination with *The Omen* movies and had satisfying dreams of being seduced by Satan, while her mother fucked a string of men in the other bedroom. She also kept in sporadic touch with the Intelligent Woman, who later introduced her to her future husband: a Heavyset Man who is also an Intelligent Man, though less intelligent than the Intelligent Woman's Intelligent Man and, while also an Academic, less successful, too.

If this were the Fat Counselor's story, the Intelligent Woman would be called the Beautiful Woman, because her hair is wild and curly and she goes barefoot with a toe ring and her toenails are always the color of blood in a vial, and she gets her hands hennaed and has a Miró tattoo in the small of her back and wears size four slinky dresses and takes ballet class (at thirty-one!) and her smile lights up a room.

But the Fat Counselor's not in Greece. She's at home being fat. So you just forget about that.

In Minneapolis, the Sister of the Beautiful Woman lives with a Slacker Boy who looks like Shaggy from *Scooby-Doo*. They are in a band and rarely smile or shower, and though the Band Sister is a Beautiful Woman, too, she hides it under buzzed hair and gaudy makeup and thrift-store boy's striped pants until the only thing the Sisters have in common is that once, within a span of two days, each was attacked and bitten by a squirrel.

In different cities, mind you. What are the chances!

The Intelligent Woman, though she has a PhD, does not have a real job. Oh, she teaches part time at a few universities and writes the occasional book review, but the money she makes yearly would barely even cover this cruise.

The Beautiful Woman works bringing coffee to Traveling Sales Reps and arranging flight and hotel accommodations for business trips that do not involve her presence, but that many of the Traveling Sales Reps imagine do.

Though everybody thinks she is a Trophy Wife, the Beautiful Woman doubts the truth of this since the Macho Man does not wish her to have a child. Most Trophy Wives bear Trophy Children, don't they? The Macho Man enjoys driving two cars and owning a lakefront condo; if they had children, the Beautiful Woman might want to quit her job and become a Dead Weight like the Intelligent

Woman, and then imagine the bills! What can the Intelligent Man be thinking, letting his Wife get away with that shit?

The Beautiful Woman is less valuable at the moment as a Mother than as a Cash Cow.

The Intelligent Woman and the Intelligent Man are in the process of adopting a Chinese Girl, because Chinese People are usually intelligent and because the Intelligent Woman is Infertile. They are excited about their forthcoming Baby. They are not the kind of people who get hung up on propagating their own genetics when there is a population problem at hand. They are happy for the chance to Do Good. Women who make such a big deal about Infertility are Stupid Dolts with Pointless Lives; Husbands who insist upon their own sperm are Narcissistic Assholes. They, however, are Intelligent People, expecting an Intelligent Baby. They are above bourgeois bullshit like that.

Are they really? Wow. *Are they really?* Hey, what do you want from me? This is what they say when asked.

Back in Madison, Wisconsin, in the private dorm full of out-of-staters like the Intelligent Woman, the Beautiful Woman, and the Aggressive Woman, hostilities brewed. One day, the Intelligent Woman was in the hallway relaying to her Gay Male Friend how the Beautiful Woman had said, Well, I don't see anybody buying you roses so you really have no right to judge, and the Beautiful Woman came out of her room and said, Don't you know that I can hear you talking about me? To which the Intelligent Woman said, So what, you said it, didn't you, so why should you care who hears? To which the Beautiful Woman replied, This is none of your business. Why don't you stop being such a gossip and butt out? After which the Intelligent Woman warned, You'd better just go back in your room, you little suburban twit, before I kick your ass.

Whereupon the Gay Male Friend exclaimed, Whoa – you can take the girl out of the neighborhood, but you can't take the neighborhood out of the girl!

To which a year of silence between the Intelligent Woman and the Beautiful Woman was the response.

In the WASP-filled Minnesota suburb where the Jewish Girl and her younger Rebel Sister lived with their Jewish Mother and German Father, the Father was the Sun around which they, female planets, revolved. The Mother was jealous of her Beautiful Daughters, because the Father was obsessed with them and thought of nothing except saving money for their security and making sure they were not hit by cars. The Rebel Sister was tired of having her arm gripped tightly by the Father every time she approached a curb, so she had her head shaved and joined a band and painted vagina-looking abstractions on the walls of her bedroom and wrote beneath them, I am obsessed. The Good Sister got a Puerto Rican Boyfriend and repeatedly injured herself on the gymnastics team. At night in their shared bathroom, the Sisters made fun of their Father and wished that he'd get off their backs – He is *such* a dork, they said. He is so lame.

But when the Rebel Sister (now the Band Sister) was eighteen, and the Mother and the Father sold their pretty house to move to Long Island and live among the Jews, the Sisters could not believe the Mother had won. The new condo had only one extra bedroom, utilized as an exercise room. In Madison and Minneapolis respectively, the Sisters cried for days.

After the Boyfriend dumped her and she became Unstable, the Beautiful Woman acquired a reputation among off-campus Jewish Frat Boys as a Blow Job Queen. For months her Girlfriends, including the Intelligent Woman, tried to keep this hurtful gossip from her, but when news inevitably trickled her way (actually, one of the five guys who lived above Taco Bell on State Street, all of whom she'd blown, told her in an effort to make her leave his apartment so he could study), the Beautiful Woman was secretly proud.

In the fluorescent lights of the cruise ship bathroom, amid giddy tales of simultaneous copulation, the Intelligent Woman glimpses old acne scars embedded along the sides of her own face, like somebody took a smooth, clean picture of the Beautiful Woman and crumpled it up tight then left it there, ravaged under the glare.

And some things—like hearing that a woman who does not receive roses has no right to an opinion in this world—are things you never get over. Even when you receive your own roses, along with diamond earrings and a Victorian house and a Baby From China and everybody seems to respect you more than the person who made that Statement to begin with. You still don't.

The Intelligent Woman's Husband turns to her and says, Aren't you going to take your top off? You're always dying to take off your top. She looks at him, so pale in the sun, his laboratory-hidden body nearly transparent, the way it looks when he's working naked in the morning after his shower, bathed in computer-glow. He has been with her on many a foreign beach – they met in France, for God's sake! – and in addition has fucked her enough times in enough ways to know that, though she is not Beautiful and knows it, she is nonetheless an exhibitionist. She cannot fool him. He stares, waiting.

(It has not occurred to the Intelligent Man that his Wife may realize he has a hankering to see the Beautiful Woman's juicy C – maybe D? – cuppers. He is too consumed by calculating that the Beautiful Woman, by far a more timid woman than his bold Wife, will only disrobe if his Wife does so first.)

The Intelligent Woman watches her Husband's eager, glowing body. Once, when she had to get an MRI for her bladder and found herself unexpectedly claustrophobic, the Intelligent Man sat in a folding chair at her feet and held her toes comfortingly until the procedure was over. Every night in their shared bed he spoons her body and breathes into her hair, and she knows her curls tickle his nose but he stays in this position anyway until she falls asleep, and neither of them call it un-Feminist. She finds that she does not want to disappoint him – hasn't he, in a sense, earned this stupid pleasure?

Men: They are like children. What can you do?

There was a period of time during which the Intelligent Woman lived in a rural college town out East, and the Beautiful Woman lived in Texas. This was shortly after college; both had relocated in order to be with men. The Intelligent Woman's Intelligent Boyfriend (now Husband) was pursuing his PhD, and the Intelligent Woman made ends meet by waitressing, and for fun answered calls on a battered women's hotline. The Beautiful Woman, meanwhile, lived with a Former Drug Dealer who was a college drop-out, worked at a gay bar, and liked to Rollerblade through the city. The Former Drug Dealer had given the Beautiful Woman her first orgasm, so naturally she was putty in his hands. At night she waited up for him at his mother's house (where they both lived) and when he returned, keyed up from all the Hot Men who wanted to convert him, they had the most amazing sex she would ever experience. By day, the Former Drug Dealer still would not go back to college, would not seek a proper job, and dropped acid before Rollerblading between speeding cars—all of which became subjects of many fights.

A Mutual College Friend who also lived in Texas (but had been born there so it was less her fault) wrote to the Intelligent Woman up East: I think that druggie is smacking her around. The Intelligent Woman was shocked. Here her friend, the Beautiful Woman whom all the Frat Boys had so pursued (the Blowjob Queen phenomenon temporarily skipped her mind), was letting herself be beaten by some Rollerblading, non-Jewish Texan! One evening when the hotline was slow, the Intelligent Woman drafted a six-page letter to the Beautiful Woman. It read, in part: You have always suffered from low self-esteem—look at how you let that ugly little Guido kiss you in Ft. Lauderdale even though you knew he was gross—but you have to get out of this relationship and learn to love yourself, because batterers never change and no woman deserves to be hit even if you *have* totally given over all your power to this loser. You are a Beautiful Woman; is that how you want your life to be? That night, the Intelligent Woman went home and made love with her Intelligent Non-Abusive Boyfriend and fantasized about being tied up (at this time, the Intelligent Man had not yet worked up the nerve to actually act out such things) and felt smug that she had done a good deed.

In Texas, the Beautiful Woman read the letter and was embarrassed, not only because the Former Drug Dealer did in fact hit her on occasion but because she knew she *did* deserve it—she had once made such a scene at the bar that he had to have the bouncer remove her, all because she was convinced he was seeing another girl. He didn't even know any other girls! All he did was Rollerblade and work in a gay bar! Once, too, she had ripped his shirt, just as she had done to the Boyfriend on Bascom Hill back in college, only the Former Drug Dealer struggled right out of his shirt and ran away from her, and she chased him down the street screaming, I blow other guys all the time! Even though it wasn't true. The Beautiful Woman read the letter from the Intelligent Woman and thought how fortunate it must be to be so certain of one's own opinions and ethics and what one will tolerate and not tolerate and exactly what to say and do to draw the line. But when she thought about the Intelligent Woman's Intelligent Boyfriend, she knew she would never date him (though she might kiss him if he tried), because he was too *nice* and would want her to be her own person and do her own thing, and men like that made her tired, too tired to even contemplate, and not at all aroused.

So for the second time in the friendship between the Intelligent Woman and the Beautiful Woman, a silence ensued. This one lasted for six months, after which the Former Drug Dealer did actually cheat on her with a woman (go figure), and the Beautiful Woman allowed herself to be stolen away by an Australian Conservative, and she and her swell Aussie met up with the Intelligent Woman and her new Intelligent Husband to see the Miró exhibition in Manhattan, which the Intelligent Woman thought was miraculous and the Beautiful Woman thought was fine, but really not all that.

Speaking of battered women's agencies (which tend to be staffed by Lesbians, do they not?), at the same time as the Beautiful Woman and the Intelligent Woman were writing or not writing to one another from the Southwest and the East respectively, back in the Midwest the Fat Counselor was trying diligently to date chicks. The sex was OK, maybe even a little better than with men; it was the romance that posed a problem. Like sometimes, she and her Partner would be dressed in their loose black slacks and eating by candlelight at a Vegetarian Restaurant, and she would feel strangely as though she were at a dress rehearsal and things were going well enough, but the audience had not yet arrived.

Of course, the Fat Counselor had always been a little in love with the Intelligent Woman, but later, when she abandoned girls and began dating the Heavyset Man she would eventually marry, she readjusted that love to the sisterly kind, which is easier for women to do than men can possibly imagine.

The Heavyset Man may also be referred to as: the Theater Major, Grizzly Adams, Nature Boy, the Heavy Drinker, the Red-Faced Man, Sensitive Man, and Man-Suffering-from-Impotence-in-Times-of-Stress.

The Aggressive Woman lives in Bogotá, Colombia, kidnapping capital of the world. Though South America is resplendent with men who physically resemble North American Guidos, she is still unmarried. Her Friends back home joke that if she were to be kidnapped, the Guerillas would pay a ransom just to have America take her back, and the Mormons she works with (Mormons in Colombia? Don't ask!) refer to her abrasive manners as Urban Humor in order to be kind.

Sometime after the cruise, let us say a year, the Intelligent Woman says to her Husband, Do you often get hard-ons for other women? And he says, No not at all. And she says, Even when we're on the beach and you see other women's bodies right there laid out in front of you? And he says, You mean like when (and says the Beautiful Woman's name) took off her top in Greece? And she, feigning shock, says, No I didn't mean *her*—you *better* not have had a hard-on then. And he says, Well I didn't. And she knows that is true because she checked, back on the beach, watched his azure trunks from behind her sunglasses, but so what? That's the lucky thing about being in one's thirties: the dick doesn't give as much away. Eroticism is in the mind anyway, she thinks, believing thirty-two is a wise age. The dick just has to calm down a little bit before men find out.

I always have a hard-on for you, the Intelligent Man adds (see, I told you he was Intelligent), and the Intelligent Woman, still playing dumb but enjoying it suddenly, says, Oooh. And they are both happy, though they do not have sex at that very moment because they are watching a documentary about Mao on A&E.

Remember those assumptions about Academics and sex? OK, so some of them are true.

In Rhodes, four Travelers lie on straw mats on rocky sand. Three are dark-skinned and blend in fairly well; the fourth, a man, is very light. One of the women sits up abruptly and looks around, then flicks off her bikini top and chucks it in the sand. She says to the darker-skinned man, Pass me some sunscreen, and he looks, registers no shock at seeing her tiny, baby-pink breasts staring back at him, and does as she commands. The pale man continues to lie on his back, sweaty T-shirt on to keep his Presbyterian skin from burning, eyes closed against the sun's glare.

Two mats away, on the other side of the darker man, the other woman sits up. Indeed, she might easily pass for Greek. She, too, pulls off her bikini top (hers must go over her head; it's a tank and somewhat awkward) and folds it neatly to lay it over her purse. She reclines again before requesting the lotion be passed to her, too.

The Intelligent Woman glances at the Beautiful Woman's breasts, which she has actually seen many times before. Yep, they are Something.

Within half an hour, the Macho Man wants to rent mopeds and tour the island, and the Intelligent Man, responding to his cue to follow as the Macho Man does when they are playing chess, says, Cool.

The women put their tops back on and off they go to sit on the backs of mopeds, arms around the solid trunks of their Husbands, hair flying in the wind. Envisioning the image each Couple will create riding, the Beautiful Woman, whose Husband is an avid Motorcyclist, is glad for the first time on the cruise to have the Husband she has.

Or maybe the Intelligent Woman only believes this.

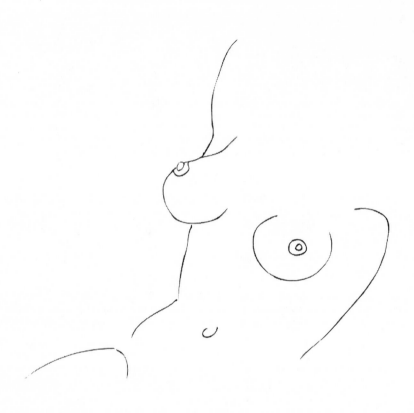

JUDY PRINCE

SUMMATE

my heart topples
in the warm caliper
of your hand,
my body a raised map—
new lines like moving silk
dance for you
long legs enfold the sea

UCHE OGBUJI

21ST CENTURY BEAUTY IN POETRY

The photograph is married to the eye,
Grafts on its bride one-sided skins of truth;
The dream has sucked the sleeper of his faith
That shrouded men might marrow as they fly.[1]

VISITING MUSÉE DU LOUVRE A FEW YEARS AGO, I MADE THE well-trodden way down the great hall to the nook of *La Joconde*, the *Mona Lisa*. Indication of just how well trodden came instantly. The corner was stuffed with tourists, almost all of them holding up digital cameras and pressing their way as far forward as they could. Luckily, I am tall and managed to see the painting at a distance of ten feet or so. I didn't try to get any closer, reasoning that I would never be able to properly appreciate the painting, anyway, in all that welter. Despite its fame, the *Mona Lisa* has never been a painting of any devotion for me. I was far more excited to see the Piero Della Francescas and Titians in that same hall, to which close access was no problem at all.

I went seeking *La Joconde* because, regardless of my lukewarm impression, derived from reproductions, I understood it to be a benchmark of well-rounded representation of beauty in art since the Renaissance. I love paintings, especially from that era, but I am no expert in those arts. I am interested in seeing the benchmarks I have received, in order to claim, at least, that these inform my aesthetic judgments and desires. What I got in Paris, as well as the hundred or so other people in the room, was a glimpse at the work much less informative than any reproduction. Some got yet more reproductions, in the form of their digital photographs. Perhaps the folks in the front got a good look, but surely this was not the bracing environment in which humans seem to best appreciate beauty. The benchmark, juxtaposed, is held abstract from us, never really fulfilling the framing role it has enjoyed throughout most of its history. This is entirely right for our age.

In our age, a prodigious number of people live in what would have been considered opulence throughout history. There is still much poverty in the world, but a staggering number of people have access to the canons in literature, music, and visual art, traveling to exotic locations, meeting a huge variety of other people throughout their lives. For many of us, however, our concepts of fineness are still derived from narrower perspective, particularly in Europe, where beauty was established in terms of Plato's forms, and the perfection of each genre established by analysis and comparison between variations in regression from forms. There is an ideal of painting, and *La Joconde* is considered closer to that ideal than most other paintings.

The entirety of Western civilization is apportioned into schools where experts conduct the process of determining closeness to the ideal. The many privileged of the world tend toward such schooling, and so when *La Joconde* hangs in the gallery, it attracts a swarm of well-drilled people eager to approach the ideal, even though the reality of the situation means that their closest approach barely improves on the abstraction of their lessons. The schools are self-limiting in their way, and it seems to me that there is a fundamental tension between beauty as defined in schools and the increasing number and diversity of people with the leisure and resources to properly contemplate these received ideals.

> Self-contained, oh Form, in the sumptuous
> Wall of violet foam you pose against
> The shaded appetite of cold mist
> And the shining touch that erects you.
>
> Thusly, Lady of dynamic repose,
> You step evenly towards your perfected sum
> Ah, like a sun, without spending in so walking
> So much as the echo of your tardy tread.[2]

Which echo brings me to poetry. Most literate people are aware of the power of poetry to express beauty, but most people are also stymied by the schools that have held sway in poetry for so long.

Most people only ever approach poetry through the same layers of abstraction through which I see *La Joconde*. It starts in childhood, where teachers no sooner put across an enjoyable poem than they trundle out the diagrams and strategies and rubrics and other destructive devices that interfere with the child's tendency to connect the original wit to their own instinctual reactions. This includes the reaction to what we consider beauty. To be fair, we've been served well by what schools have advanced for centuries in terms of how poetry connects us immediately to beauty. But in the numbers and diversity of our age, the inevitable tensions have done much to abstract away what power poetry has to allow us to express or capture the experience of beauty. Living in the middle of the phenomenon, it's not easy to find perspective to relieve such tensions and restore poetry to its native place in our pantheon, but it never hurts to look, and the arrow of time has given us a singular direction. What can the history of beauty in poetry tell us about its future?

I tend to think, as Kierkegaard and others did, that in *The Republic* Plato had his tongue partly in cheek while writing into the mouth of Socrates such stern limitations on poets. Not everyone read it that way; schools from ancient times seized upon Plato's rather zealous (taken literally) ideas in *The Republic*:

> Our artists should be those with the gift of discerning the
> true nature of the beautiful, the graceful. Then our youth
> will live in a land of health, amid fair sights and sounds,
> and receive the good inherent in all things; and beauty,
> which flows from all good things, shall flow into the eye

and ear, like a salutary breeze from a pure land, and compel
the soul from its earliest age into sympathy with the beauty
of reason.

The sanctimony of schools is written pretty heavily into this pas-
sage. There is the prejudice of a thin veil between health and physi-
cal beauty and moral luster (resurrected in its most startlingly literal
sense in the bigotry of the popular film *300*).[3] There is the concept
of truest nature, the ideal of beauty (meeting healthy opposition in
the West as long ago as Boccaccio and Rabelais with their grotesque-
aesthetic response to idealized poetry, and onward to the "coxcomb
impudence" of how Whistler kicked open the door for abstract art
in the West). There is the notion of the blessed land (debunked by
experience of desperate conflicts between heritage and calling among
immigrants who have shaped the past couple of centuries). And ulti-
mately, there is the notion of the beauty of reason, a divine, mathe-
matically continuous order over all things, radiating in all directions,
attenuating so that any person and thing that does not press toward
the ideal is left cold and dark.

> That wondrous pattern, wheresoe'er it be,
> Whether in earth laid up in secret store,
> Or else in heaven, that no man may it see
> With sinful eyes, for fear it to deflore,
> Is perfect Beauty, which all men adore;
> Whose face and feature doth so much excel
> All mortal sense, that none the same may tell.

> Thereof as every earthly thing partakes
> Or more or less, by influence divine,
> So it more fair accordingly it makes,
> And the gross matter of this earthly mine,
> Which clotheth it, thereafter doth refine,
> Doing away the dross which dims the light
> Of that fair beam which therein is empight.[4]

No one silly enough to drink too literally of Platonism ever produced any poetry worth preserving (despite my quoting of Spenser, he knew better in most of his work), but its effects meant that even those with the lyrical craft and style to write great poetry, the dead white males who have become the bogeymen of their own schools in the past fifty years, lost their relevancy through one-dimensional aesthetics. If we no longer recognize their own pious absolutes of beauty, we lose any compulsion to seek out the power of their words. This leaves a vacuum into which it's easy for charlatans to enter, and the twentieth century had quite the run of poetic charlatans. This species can always find a rich vein in some fad or another, but ultimately they lose the public.

Beauty is by no means the only thing that compels people to write poetry, or which people seek in reading poetry, but in many ways it seems the quality that has been most clearly lost from popular interaction with poetry as the tensions of modernism have played out. I believe that an important step in restoring poetry to relevance is to tap into the great crafts of classical poetry worldwide, because these are what lead people to seek out language that they themselves might not be able to express, that helps them savor and preserve their sensual experiences. The trick will be to look backward for craft while remaining true to the complexity of modern aesthetics.

If the marbled highway from *The Republic* eventually gave way to fallow wilderness in the twentieth century, and we accept that the idea of a straight-and-narrow causeway is obsolete, how do we find what we love best, as we make our new way, dispersed in all directions? For my part, the poetry with which I'm most familiar outside the radiating paths from New York, London, and Paris is African poetry, but I hope that in contemplating these thoughts, the reader can substitute the emerging traditions that most suit his or her own identity.

For better or for worse, identity has always been bound viscerally to appearance, and idealized beauty has always been feted by Western poets, notably in *la dompna soiseubuda* of the troubadours, the "borrowed lady" assembled from parts of individual women seen in their ideal form, looking back to Rufinus.

> Melite, yours are eyes of Hera, hands of Athena,
> Breasts of Aphrodite, ankles of Thetis.
> He is happy who beholds you, thrice happy who
> hears you,
> A demi-god who kisses you, and immortal who shares
> your bed.[5]

Then there was Dante's Platonic abstract of Beatrice, whose beauty was more the knot in the hyperbola of God's order than anything bound to real life, and then Petrarca's Laura, far less ethereal than Beatrice, given the poet's clear, personal exploration, but no more earthy. Earthy came along with Boccaccio's Griseida, at which point the stereotype made a start toward including even real women the writer knew. Of course, this realness came with an undercurrent of contempt, which carried through to Villon where his extremely earthy women nevertheless did not often range beyond "orde paillarde" ("filthy slut"). In England, poets expressed their own passions within the chivalrous orders of neo-Platonism from Chaucer through Herrick, with his famous poems for the possibly imaginary (and certainly idealized) Julia.

As for descriptions of beauty in men, this was clearly shaky ground, despite the extent to which the ancient Greeks reveled in such descriptions. Much European description reaching to Adonis as ideal has had a decidedly effeminate touch. Yes, there are effeminate, beautiful men, but once again the type was restricted to a tiny fragment of the actual species. You start to feel the spectrum expand among nineteenth-century French poets, but perhaps it was not until Whitman that we got a reasonably broad approach to the aesthetics of man-flesh. Perceived beauty of men's souls, however, was much more vigorously engaged and didn't seek the absolute bond between physical beauty and good that reached its apex in characterization of women with Dante. Aesthetics compatible with same-sex romance is just another frontier into which poetry in the twenty-first century will continue to expand.

As poetry expands into such frontiers, it will finally begin to catch up to the diversity of real men and women, almost certainly with greater speed than Hollywood, where within the span of a single century Mae West slew the Gibson Girl, and then came Ursula

Andress and Liz Taylor, and now Halle Berry, Gong Li, Jessica Alba, and Aishwarya Rai from Hollywood, Bollywood, and Hong Kong. The public is dominated by the aesthetics of artfully photographed and airbrushed leading stars whose main livelihood is beauty and fitness training. The sprawl of the supermarket magazine rack is far more influential through ubiquity than the occasional glimpse of a princess on her litter passing in the street in olden days, and this reality has driven so much of the modern anxiety over image of beauty. I think a lot of this anxiety is misplaced, and that the Hollywood example shows how rapidly precepts are evolving as diversity takes root in the population itself. But where is the poetry that celebrates this evolution in personal beauty?

> I wanted to write you a letter
> my love
> a letter of intimate secrets
> a letter of memories of you
> of you
> your lips as red as the tacula fruit
> your hair black as the black diloa fish
> your eyes as gentle as the macongue
> your breasts hard as young maboque fruit ...[7]

There is plenty of poetry that expresses the anxiety, even of dubious desirousness. Suheir Hammad warns:

> Don't seduce yourself with my
> Otherness
> the beat of my lashes

against each other ain't some
dark desert beat it's just
a blink get over it.[8]

There is an entire institution of poets concerned about girls confused in consciousness of their appearance, offering these endangered an aesthetic that does not offend their mirror.

where I stand whole/deconstructing
past nicknames
like zebra, mutt or half-n-half
while remembering my father
held me through 11-year-old
tears calling me by name
calling me beautiful
Now, some say
must be Black
could be white
maybe she's pinay
Add Mexican to the list
Puerto Rican
tan white girl
Are you from the South?
Or the best one yet
Are you Egyptian?[9]

Even some of the greatest paeans to non-European beauty in the past century seem laced with anguish.

Bare lady, dark lady
Ripe fruit of firm flesh, somber ecstasies of black wine,
mouth that inclines
My mouth lyrical
Savannah of pure horizons, savannah that stirs to the fervent caresses of
the Westerly Wind
Carved tomtom, taut tomtom which groans under fingers
of the Conqueror
Your deep contralto voice is the spirit chant of the Beloved.[10]

Plato's marker passage includes the concept of purer regions, which send healthy breezes about. The usual Greek inspiration for such paragon country was the province of Arcadia, and *The Republic* itself expanded upon such a tourist's interest, gilding it into a complete utopia of ways as well as vistas. Utopia before and after Sir Thomas More gave it its name, has remained a topic large in Western poetry, rarely treated with more effect than by Coleridge.

And there were gardens bright with sinuous rills,
Where blossomed many an incense-bearing tree;
And here were forests ancient as the hills,
Enfolding sunny spots of greenery.[11]

The draw to the pole of Plato is so strong that critics have developed an elaborate system of how the iconic locales of this poem are analogous with poetry itself. But of course Coleridge merely mentioned an exotic Chinese locale and threw in the likes of Abyssinia as if it wasn't clear that he really meant Arcadia. Such blinkered confusion was every bit as common in descriptions of the New World until its denizens undertook descriptions themselves.

> Water sensual, slow as molasses,
> sugar port, torrid bay,
> with the light in repose
> scudding the clean waves,
> and the drowsy murmur of beehives
> congealed from the bustlings about shore.
> […]
> With voiced parts of the Song of Songs,
> You are brown because the sun watches you.[12]

And the same can be said of Africa, for which you need not look any further than the ridiculous descriptions Joseph Conrad reports from the mind of his characters. Yet even when Africans thrust forth their own poetry in colonial tongues, they did so with their own dystopian bent fueled by outrage over colonialism. Africa among twentieth-century African poets is a bleak landscape that I certainly do not recognize insofar as I've traveled the real continent.

How much changed in perceptions when Europe evolved from the vanity of the Ptolemaic universe, with Earth at the center through the spheres to God upon the outer *primum mobile*, to the contemporary idea of Earth as "pale blue dot" among the "billions and billions" of Carl Sagan's famous expressions. Or more topically, as the map of the world evolved from medieval to the modern globe, and now Google Earth all the way down to Street View.

For far above these heavens, which here we see,
Be others far exceeding these in light,
Not bounded, not corrupt, as these same be,
But infinite in largeness and in height,
Unmoving, uncorrupt, and spotless bright,
That need no sun t' illuminate their spheres,
But their own native light far passing theirs.

And as these heavens still by degrees arise,
Until they come to their first Mover's bound,
That in his mighty compass doth comprise,
And carry all the rest with him around;
So those likewise do by degrees redound,
And rise more fair; till they at last arrive
To the most fair, whereto they all do strive.

Fair is the heaven where happy souls have place,
In full enjoyment of felicity,
Whence they do still behold the glorious face
Of the divine eternal Majesty;
More fair is that, where those Ideas on high
Enranged be, which Plato so admired,
And pure Intelligences from God inspired.[13]

But how does the concept of an ideal land, that eternal other country, work into a world where people come and go to lands the world over? Our cosmopolitan age stymies the idea of a universal ideal of ultimate beauty of any land, either in its nature or in its society. The dystopias that especially became popular in the twentieth century express the anxiety that utopia implies a dangerous level of forced conformity. I once read a classic science-fiction story in a utopian setting, described in terms of a scientific discovery of dimensional partitioning so that each person could live in an endless realm of his own choosing, alone or grouped as he desired. Such a solipsistic idea of isolated utopia is maybe closest to reality in terms of modern social networks, where we can adopt identities of our choosing, connect with fellows of our choosing, and even adopt simulated lives as farmers, vampires, mafiosi, mages, or what we like. It's one foot into a William Gibson universe, but it's worth remembering that even Gibson's universes were dystopian in consequence.

I am not one of those with deep-seated anxiety about the fact that current generations spend so much time in virtual worlds. Nevertheless, for better or for worse, such worlds are an enormous part of modern life, and where is the poetry that describes these solipsistic worlds of virtually configured existence? Where is the poetry that allows us to reflect our own visions of beauty that we perceive through this shattered mirror? In the idioms of the day, our configuration of virtual living is a remix of life, and then a remix of the remixes. Perhaps it's as simple as the idea that we might tend toward remix poetry. Certainly much of the poetry that remains popular today, from Slam to Def Poetry Jam, is heavy on remix themes and laden with the corresponding hip-hop style. Twenty-first-century poets will be charged with taking all the various approaches to beauty in the various ages and cultures they encounter, related to the various places and people in real and virtual worlds. It seems inevitable that there will come about tools to select and rework sentiments and passages that express what we love. Indeed, how might a GarageBand for poetry function?

This is a less fanciful question than it might seem. In the early twentieth century, the mechanical invention was the shift-key typewriter, and Hugh Kenner among other critics have pointed out how the stalwarts of that era such as Ezra Pound and W.C. Williams were influenced by that invention. Charles Olson famously compared the effect of the typewriter on the poet to that of the stave and bar on the musician. This is not even to mention concrete and other visual poetry. The typewriter, however, did no more than amplify the contemporary conceptual invention, that of collage style. Some of the most celebrated poems of the twentieth century, including "The Wasteland" and "The Cantos," were largely collage of other verse and references, cryptically juxtaposed using what glue came from the poet's store of inspiration. Much of this work carried the age's typical dystopian flavor, as if to say: "Here are all these many worlds, compiled for you, and see? It's still but a rotting mess."

HERE YOU OBSERVE THE RUMP OF PLATONISM, WITH ITS IDEA of inherent good in all things, and the concept of inner, intrinsic beauty versus what is perceived through the senses. This spirit inevitably informed the poetic schools of those days, especially as poets found echoes not just from Greek but also from other cultural keystone texts, such as Chinese, Japanese, or Persian poetry and philosophy, The Vedas and Upanishads.

As Kenner points out, Ezra Pound was a leading docent in this school, and in one of the great passages in one of the great poems of his century, he decried the clearly evolving aesthetics of the modern age:

> Even the christian beauty
> Defects, after Samothrace.
> we see τὸ καλόν
> decreed in the marketplace[14]

But this complaint marks precisely where Pound's genius was grafted to his folly. He too often started with a brilliant insight, that the glories of art derive more from pure fervor and inspiration than from base motives such as profit, and took such insight to the extreme; for example, decrying any say of the marketplace in our understanding of beauty. In an article contemplating Pound's iconic Canto XLV "With Usura" in the context of the financial meltdown of 2008, I wrote:

> Pound argues that ideally [the smallholder, master crafts-man's] profit lies in direct commerce to the buyer, and not a mass production that drowns craft. When you are selling to ten thousand it is less about the personal palate, the long-negotiated boundaries of community or the carefully-measured cut of cloth. It's all about the race to the average, to the mediocre, to the safe rather than the cunning. It's not "commerce is evil," but rather "petty commerce is the richest and most enduring commerce."[15]

Even before the heyday of Madison Avenue, Pound saw the power and peril of the marketplace decree in beauty, and saw that it would swamp the ideals of the old schools, but he went too far in assuming this implied a destruction of aesthetic good. What he missed is that the marketplace means a negotiation of what is beautiful. That such constant negotiation offers more richness and vibrancy than the diktat of any particular school. Ezra Pound feared the Walmart of beauty but missed the trick that the same basic capitalism also ensures an Etsy of beauty.

An Etsy[16] of beauty in language is perhaps exactly what the twenty-first century of poetry will be about. The search and navigation tools, the community ratings, the poet who gets swept to fame possibly on the wave of a meme, and better yet on slowly accrued recognition of merit. The commerce of physical and virtual world brings to mind less a rigid Ptolemaic construction than good old Parliament/Funkadelic Cosmic Slop.

And this would seem to be the natural consequence of the twentieth century. What was beauty under the diamond sky of LSD? What was beauty after we'd nuked the Bikini Atoll? It's not as if there are no more fears left to us. What is beauty under threat of terrorism or environmental collapse or climate change? What was beauty once we'd visited the black desert of the moon and watched the iconic Earthrise? Once we'd for the first time had a chance to see the blue-white abstraction of our own planet from afar?

Around the same time as Pound's fierce reaction, a Persian poet was assembling ranged banalities that would later prove so concordant with the hippie mind, touching on beauty among other things.

And beauty is not a need but an ecstasy.
It is not a mouth thirsting nor an empty hand
stretched forth,
But rather a heart enflamed and a soul enchanted.
It is not the image you would see nor the song you
would hear,
But rather an image you see though you close your eyes
and a song you hear though you shut your ears.
It is not the sap within the furrowed bark, nor a wing
attached to a claw,
But rather a garden forever in bloom and a flock of angels
for ever in flight.

People of Orphalese, beauty is life when life unveils her
holy face.
But you are life and you are the veil.
Beauty is eternity gazing at itself in a mirror.
But you are eternity and you are the mirror.[17]

Diversity needn't mean diffuse thinking. The slop is what you
see from a million miles away, but what we actually use will be
immediate and clear. I think these coming generations will demand
more concrete expressions of beauty, without necessarily collapsing
to the old absolutes. As in so many modern trends in poetry, Hop-
kins is still exceptionally relevant in how he shows how the language
of such things can be intensely personal without losing the breadth
of its expressive power.

Glory be to God for dappled things—
For skies of couple-colour as a brinded cow;
For rose-moles all in stipple upon trout that swim;
Fresh-firecoal chestnut-falls; finches' wings;
Landscape plotted and pieced—fold, fallow, and plough;
And áll trádes, their gear and tackle and trim.[18]

And one day, around 2050, a young girl will be sitting in an eco-diverse canopy forest (preserved despite all the dire warnings of environmental apocalypse), admiring all the components of her leaf-shadowed scene, and she'll turn on her wrist-top computer and tune in for poetry to match her sentiment. And she will find a paean composed by an earlier poet who happened to be sitting a decade earlier in the very same location, and she'll savor the poem, with her thrill of discovery and her satisfaction in its aptness. And maybe, as she clicks on "related poems," she will stumble across "Pied Beauty." And spreading across her face in that moment perhaps the enigmatic smile of *La Joconde*. And even Plato, I'm sure, would not be able to begrudge her the moment.

ENDNOTES

1. From "Our Eunuch Dreams," by Dylan Thomas (1934).

2. From "Presencia y fuga," by José Gorostiza (1939), translated by Uche Ogbuji.

3. I might also mention Emerson's "Beauty is the mark God sets upon virtue," against which we can balance Tolstoy's calling a delusion any connection between beauty and goodness.

4. From "A Hymn in Honour of Beauty," by Edmund Spenser. "empight:" placed.

5. Epigram xxxv, by Rufinus. For "Aphrodite" Rufinus uses her epithet "The Paphian," but I substitute the common name of the goddess.

6. From "Letter from a Contract Worker" in *When Bullets Begin to Flower*, by Antonio Jacinto (1972), translated by Margaret Dickinson. "Macongue": henna dye. "Maboque": wild orange.

7. From "Exotic," by Suheir Hammad, from *Born Palestinian, Born Black* (Harlem River Press, 1996).

8. From "A Mixed Message," by Tara Betts (1999).

9. From "Femme Noire," by Léopold Sédar Senghor (1977), trans. Uche Ogbuji.

10. "Eres la tierra verdadera, el aire / Que siempre quiere el pecho respirar." from "Patria," by Roberto Fernández Retamar (1974). "You are the true land, the air the breast ever yearns to breathe."

11. From "Kublai Khan," by Samuel Taylor Coleridge (1816).

12. From "Mulata-Antilla," by Luis Palés Matos (1950), trans. Uche Ogbuji.

> Agua sensual y lenta de melaza,
> puerto de azúcar, cálida bahía,
> con la luz en reposo
> dorando la onda limpia,
> y el soñoliento zumbo de colmena
> que cuajan los trajines de la orilla.
> [...]
> Con voces del Cantar de los Cantares,
> eres morena porque el sol te mira.

13. From "An Hymn of Heavenly Beauty," by Edmund Spenser, a different poem from the earlier cited.

14. From "Hugh Selwyn Mauberley," by Ezra Pound (1920). τὸ καλόν ("TO KALON") means "the beautiful." Samothrace is the Greek island, ancient host to a cult of beauty, and excavation site of the famous Nike statue at the Louvre.

15. "Only one poem for the implosion of Capital," by Uche Ogbuji, *The Nervous Breakdown*, April 2009.

16. "Etsy is a social commerce Web site focused on handmade or vintage items as well as art and craft supplies. These items cover a wide range, including art, photography, clothing, jewelry, edibles, bath & beauty products, quilts, knick-knacks, and toys. Many individuals also sell craft supplies like beads, wire, jewelry-making tools, and much more." http://en.wikipedia.org/wiki/Etsy.

17. From "Beauty xxv" in *The Prophet*, by Khalil Gibran (1918).

18. From "Pied Beauty," by Gerard Manley Hopkins (1877).

CATHERINE TUFARIELLO

MEDITATION IN MIDDLE AGE

Beauty is youth, youth beauty; that is all,
A truth that you can straight-arm or embrace
When eyes slide past you, and your mother's face
Looks from the mirror, mirror on the wall.
With or without knives, needles, lasers, dyes,
You'll lose this war. But losses can be freeing,
And there were things you missed while locked in seeing
Yourself, in your mind's eye, through others' eyes.

Intent now, you're startled by the shimmer
Of stars and landscapes swimming from a blur
Of burned-off fog. And you're the child you were,
Intent and self-forgetful. See her curled
Unnoticed on a window seat in summer,
Lost in the dew-sharp garden of the world.

This poem was also published in the e-zine *Mezzo Cammin*, Summer 2011.

RONLYN DOMINGUE

MILKWEED AND METAMORPHOSIS

S HE KNEW WHAT SHE WAS DOING, THAT QUIRKY NATIVE-PLANT lady at the farmers' market.

Every weekend, she stood behind her table filled with exotic-looking flowers and shrubbery. Never mind that they grew in untouched profusion in various parts of the state. Few nurseries carried hearty Louisiana swamp irises, American beautyberry, or Joe Pye weed. Unfamiliar to so many eyes, most plants in the containers had laminated signs with photos of mature blooms and foliage, sun requirements, soil preferences, and peak bloom months.

For years, I cultivated a traditional sense of aesthetics, what a proper garden should look like, what familiar plants belonged in groups together. My perception of beauty shifted when I saw my first Indian Pink. Clusters of crimson throats with yellow screams. I desired that wild exuberance, that fierce unexpectedness of color and texture, that proper nourishment for insects and animals. The plant lady fed my fix and my soul.

I coveted some native milkweed to add to our butterfly garden. Our neighbors, one block away, had a non-native patch in their front yard that had been devoured to the stem bases two years prior. That year, it was making a comeback. Prancing groups of monarchs brought delight at a distance, but the caterpillars would require closer proximity.

On the plant lady's table that morning, I spied a lone milkweed plant, home to two tiny yellow-and-black-striped caterpillars. One was the length of an almond, the other stumpy as a kidney bean. The emotional manipulation was genius. Who could resist something *that* cute?

"Look," I said to my partner, Todd, "two caterpillars."

The sight of them triggered an old memory. I had read a book when I was little about a girl who watched a monarch caterpillar become a butterfly. She had a milkweed field outside of her house (I recall...) where the butterflies twirled, fed, and laid their eggs. She placed a caterpillar in a glass enclosure, gave it as much milkweed it could eat, and witnessed its topsy-turvy disappearing act into a chrysalis. Days later, the green jewel split open. She released the monarch into the field.

Deep down, I never forgot my envy of what she saw.

My adult hands grabbed the milkweed. I asked for more information about soil needs, to which the plant lady replied it would live in almost anything. Good, because the butterfly garden's soil structure was evolving from barren to adequate, with the potential for fertile.

That morning, I set the milkweed in the ground and gave it plenty of water. The caterpillars twitched their black antennae, kept their feet firm on the undersides of leaves. Leaves. Food. Oh no.

In my glee and enthusiasm, I failed to realize the one twelve-inch plant could not possibly sustain two ravenous caterpillars until they were ready for their next life stage. The following few hours of my life were a mission to save the babies.

I knew monarch butterflies fed on the nectar of many flowers but that their young ate only one thing—milkweed. Although I'd decided to go native in our yard—restoring a balance and beauty progress had thwarted—it would be impossible to get more of the native variety in time to spare the caterpillars.

Plan A. Contact neighbors. With luck, they might have a couple of plants to dig up and sustain our little friends. No one answered when I called, so I left a message that bordered on crazy, certified as eccentric.

"Hi, A— and J—, this is your neighbor, Ronlyn Domingue. You know, the one in the modern house. I'm calling because I just bought a milkweed plant with two baby caterpillars on it, and I realized they don't have enough to eat. So I'd like to know if you have some extra milkweed growing this year and if I can stop by to dig up a little bit. Please give me a call when you get a chance. Thanks."

I half-seriously pondered a quick visit, shovel in hand, whether or not they were home. No, that was likely criminal—and bizarre.

Plan B. Buy more plants. A few minutes online yielded a list of milkweed species that were monarch host plants. One had a common name—butterfly weed—which I recalled seeing in local nurseries. Gas prices and time being at a premium, I began to call around town. None in stock here, shipment late there, finally – success. My garbled Latin name pronunciation, with accurate spelling, matched what a nursery staff person thought they had out on tables at that moment.

Todd and I drove across town to find a stash of plants that looked like the one we'd put in the ground. The containers had the name of the nursery where the plants were propagated, located less than a two-hour drive from where we lived. I wondered whether the milkweed was native – that would have been a boon – but right then, all I cared was that the plants were healthy and large enough to survive their inevitable defoliation.

We had our own little milkweed patch by early afternoon. The caterpillars munched unaware of the drama, content to doze and grow, eat and eliminate, crawl and shed their too-small skins.

MAY RAINED PURPLE PLUMS FROM THE SOLITARY TREE. A twice-daily harvest, gathered off the ground, kept the rot under control. Morning and afternoon, I picked plums. Morning, afternoon, and several times in between, I checked on Cater and Fatter Cater.

Clever names, I know. Cater must have been a day or two younger than Fatter Cater, who clearly outpaced its sibling or cousin in length and width. They consumed their original milkweed, leaving only a pencil-thick green stalk behind. Each had chosen its own host plant to continue its binge.

They didn't do much, but they were endlessly entertaining. Leaves disappeared from the tips to the petioles in minute bites. Their little faces bobbed as they chewed, nodding with determination, maybe even contentment. Once all the green had been chewed from respective stems, they'd march their plump feet down the stalk and reach out above the ground in search of the next stash of food. Sometimes, they attached under a large leaf, panting, if caterpillars can pant, as if exhausted from their activities. This subtle repetitive motion is what wriggled them free from old skins. Their skins fell in crunched, tight coils shaped like tiny misshapen rings. If touched or stroked, they flinched. Minutely huggable as they appeared, the caterpillars wished to be left alone.

Approximately ten days after their arrival in our garden, Fatter Cater vanished. Cater went about its business unaware or unconcerned. I, however, was not nonchalant. Todd received an e-mail update that the bigger one was missing. I wondered if Fatter Cater had become a bird's bitter breakfast or a cat's plaything. Although I didn't know how many days elapsed between hatching and pupa stage (about two weeks, incidentally), I thought Fatter Cater seemed rather large and likely ready to begin its next phase.

I went back outside in search of Fatter Cater. It wasn't built for walking, and I didn't think it could get that far too fast, what with leaves, sticks, plants, and a stray brick or two in the way. With soft stealthy steps of which a ninja would have been proud, I crept around the milkweed and nearby herbs. I shifted my focus as best I could – even a striped caterpillar had the power of camouflage in its defense – and looked for movement rather than color.

There, in the parsley thicket, was the intrepid Fatter Cater.

"Where are you going?" I asked it. "Shouldn't you stay near your plant?"

No doubt, Fatter Cater's mysterious biological clock had ticked into adolescence. Lucky for it, a time to be spent cocooned and asleep. I coaxed it onto a twig and relocated it under a gnawed milk-weed. Visions of green bejeweled chrysalises dangled across my mind's eye. I coveted one of my very own.

I didn't feel right about placing it in a glass container to wait out its emergence. I had no qualms, at the moment, about closing it off around the milkweed. How does one contain a caterpillar?

Veil netting. I had plenty of it.

Past the butterfly garden and plum tree was a struggling young persimmon which had survived neglect and Hurricane Katrina. It grew the tenderest pastel green leaves that became darker and larger by the week yet remained just as succulent. Something feasted on it every night, threatened its survival. One night before bed, Todd and I went outside to see if we could identify the insect that left delicate chomp marks on the leaves. We swept a branch with a flashlight's beam. June bugs.

"What's that clicking sound?" Todd asked.

I leaned in to watch one nibble-nibble and heard its tiny mandibles clack against each other. The sight and sound was sort of funny, sort of horrifying. I picked the June bugs off with my hands and dropped them on the ground. One or two buzzed by and missed their landings. Dinner had some luck involved. The following day, I bought five yards of veil netting to cover the persimmon and several young shrubs that showed signs of June bug bites.

So it was the persimmon's netting that I borrowed to trap Fat-ter Cater and Cater. I angled a few dead branches to provide places on which they could latch. I draped the netting over the milkweed, branches, and several herbs and held it down with old bricks. They weren't going anywhere.

Curious about this stage in their growth, I went online to learn more. What I discovered made me go back outside and free them.

When a monarch caterpillar is ready to pupate, it will walk several yards away from its host plant. It will seek a sheltered area to anchor itself and enshroud within a chrysalis. Monarch caterpillars have been doing that for thousands of years, long before humans had glass jars and curious intentions.

Fatter Cater was only doing what Nature willed, what its nature knew to do. As much as I wanted to watch it transform in real time before my eyes—no photos, no time-lapse video—I knew I had to respect its instinct. I had to let it go.

Fatter Cater was gone by the next morning, Cater two days later. Although I circled the yard and peered into bushes and under eaves, I found no sign of them.

THE NEXT SUMMER WE PLANTED THREE MORE MILKWEEDS. Clusters of red-orange nectar-filled goblets grew on the tips of the spindly green stalks. A monarch appeared once in a while but never a playful group dizzy with life.

There was hope, though.

One July afternoon, I stepped outside for a short break. The summer had been dry and hot, too brutal to bother with a garden that was, as intended, taking care of itself. I lingered to inspect aphids, yellow and gooey among one group of milkweed blossoms. A half-grown caterpillar twitched its antenna at me. Nearby, a smaller one rested under a flawless leaf. And farther down, another... until I checked every plant and counted nineteen caterpillars from the newly hatched, small as a thistle seed to the nearly grown.

They ate. They grew. They disappeared. Not one stayed close enough to honor me with a view of its metamorphosis, its secret brilliant breath into flight.

Milkweed is perennial. It will return year after year until the plants exhaust themselves. Our yard is part of the monarch's flight path, their genetic memory. They'll be back, too.

With each butterfly's arrival, there's a chance for me to be the adult incarnation of the little girl in the picture book I once loved.

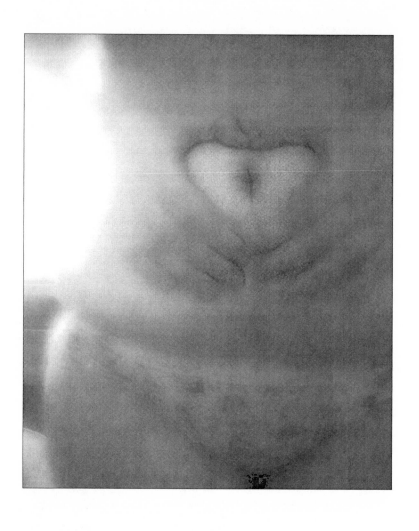

STEPHANIE ST. JOHN

BELLY UP

My whole life, I've had a belly.

There's a picture of me as a baby on the changing table; there I am, Popeye and her belly. Another photograph shows me at age four at the pool. You can see it in our photo album: me, a two-piece, and my rolls of belly (I haven't worn a bikini since).

In middle school, I learned to suck it in. I had to, because back then, we wore designer jeans so tight you needed pliers to zip them. (They needed to have that painted-on look, that nothing-comes-between-me-and-my-Calvins look.) Don't get me wrong—just because I managed to pour myself into my Sassons does not mean I was ever tiny. But the Buddha remained hidden.

I come from a long line of baby-making, D-cup, wide-hipped, short n' curvy ladies. But unlike my predecessors, whose paradigm of feminine form was Marilyn Monroe's hourglass, I was competing with Charlie's Angels.

Plus, back then, it wasn't exactly easy to diet. There were no Whole Foods or Trader Joe's. Pilates and yoga were not ubiquitous. There were no abs – eight-minute or otherwise. All we had to work with was Tab, Sweet'N Low, Alba shakes, Weight Watchers pizza, Dexatrim, cigarettes, and good old-fashioned starvation.

But anorexia was not appealing to me. My mother had an eating disorder, and she wound up rotting her teeth, losing her hair, and messing up her eyes. My teeth, hair, and eyes are my good features. I didn't want to kill the belly at their expense. Yet my attitude toward the Buddha changed. Instead of a soft friend that gave me comfort, my belly became my enemy.

The night before I lost my virginity, I took a hand mirror to my bed to see what the best angle would be for "doing it" – the flattest-stomach angle. (Can you guess what the best position was?) Belly as Enemy became a mind-set that continued for the next twenty years – until the day I read the magic word on the home pregnancy test that I carried into the bedroom in our tiny New York apartment that fateful morning.

We're going to have a baby! Inside me was a swelling. And a sense of deep inner relaxation.

Suddenly, I found myself rubbing my hands across my belly. It was going to get big. I was going to get big. My flattish (but never all the way flat) belly was now, gasp, too small!

I wanted it big. For the first time, I wanted strangers to notice my belly; I wanted it to be seen and felt. I wanted it to be filled with nourishing food that would give my growing baby a smart brain and a perfectly-fused-together spine. I was suddenly aware that every-thing I breathed, drank, and ate would go directly to my amazing pod inside. Five apples and a jar of peanut butter? To the baby! A pint of mint chocolate chip Häagen-Dazs? Hey, it's what the baby wants!

A friend of mine, who'd already had her two children and proclaimed her done-ness, gave me an overflowing bin of maternity clothes at the start of my second trimester. I opened that bin unaware of the treasures that lay waiting inside. After sifting through several cute shirts and a scarily large bathing suit, the most amazing creation I had ever seen landed across my lap: the maternity jean. Lordy lord! Where that cold metal zipper and dauntingly thick button once dug into my skin was the most glorious thing I'd ever seen: a big blue band of stretch fabric, to give room for and cradle my ever-expanding belly. How had I not known of such a thing before? No wonder pregnant ladies are glowing; they're finally relaxed! They're finally allowed to stop sucking in their guts and let that Buddha breathe!

My face was lean, my chin was single, my caloric intake went right to the baby ... ahhh. Unlike the other moms in my prenatal yoga class, I didn't worry about gaining weight. They would talk of doctors who scolded them for eating too much cheese. My midwife knew better. She was trying to keep me relaxed and happy so that when I went into labor, I'd just push my little guy right out (and that's a whole other story; oy). Besides, these were petite women, not hip to the Way of the Belly. They already worried about how their bodies would look after pregnancy. I was too happy being allowed to have a big belly to care about later. Breastfeeding burns five hundred calories a day! I wore maternity jeans and ate whatever I wanted and didn't gain anything but baby.

Pregnancy had provided me with an unexpected benefit: belly freedom.

Six years later, with a Lego-obsessed six-year-old son and a four-year-old daughter who talks back and grazes like a farm animal, I am proud to say that I no longer wear anything maternity. But I did for a while, probably more than what is condoned in certain social circles. (It's a great day when you are the giver of the bin to another newly pregnant lady who has yet to discover the wonder of the maternity jean.)

I still have my belly, just as I did before. I've daydreamed about getting a tummy tuck. It's tempting. If I had the money, maybe I would. But I don't want to die getting a cosmetic elective surgery. How horrible would that be, to die because you can't accept yourself, because your hotness is (literally) a matter of life and death? Sorry, too much to live for. And while I recovered, I wouldn't be able to pick up my kids and go sledding with them and roll all over the floor with them for months. Months are the equivalent of years to the kids. So I daydream about my tummy tuck until more important things tug at my sleeve, interrupt my sleep, and demand my soft-bellied love and attention.

RICH FERGUSON

NO ANIMALS OR INSECTS WERE TORTURED OR KILLED IN THE MAKING OF THIS POEM

WHAT I WANT: TO CRANK CREATION'S CONTRAST KNOB TO fully illuminate what's right about the world.

I wanna be Faith's strung-out junkie. My dreaming veins singing a better tomorrow.

What I don't want: to be dust, rust. Roadtripping with demons—Oblivion or bust.

Don't wanna be that one suicide bullet locked and loaded in the chamber of grief's gun. Don't wanna be your blood-lusting grave, your ghost-moan grave, your any kinda grave.

What I want: to spend time in your joy's city. I'll sweep the streets, round up criminals, direct traffic – anything and everything to keep your bliss vibrant and alive.

I wanna radioactivate, self-immolate. Burn away all poverty, fear, and sickness to fuel the fire of our well-being.

Don't wanna be an inert gas in the Idiotic Table of Elements. Wanna be a full-on kick in the balls to ignorance.

Never wanna torture or kill any animals or insects in the making of these words, these beliefs, no matter how low I may get between thought, between breath, between life and death.

But if anything must die, let it be the ego. Let it go.

What I want: for you to write on my flesh everything you see and hear when you sleep. Wanna believe the pen outlasts the blade. Freedom outlasts the chains.

I wanna shred your self-doubt, refold it into a confident origami.

Wanna see you go out into the night, take a deep breath. Sip in stars, planets, moonbeams. Let me visit the solar system in your head. Let me be asteroid, nebula. Let us become the Universe of We.

Don't wanna be old news, worn-out shoes, poorly played blues. Don't wanna be a perpetual cruiser up and down the Boulevard of Bad Vibes.

I wanna shake our collective birthright of shame, blame. Want the veins in my hands to be Sanskrit letters spelling out the words: "I will hold you up when you're down."

I wanna believe that had we lived in the Warsaw Ghetto, we would've been survivors. We would've been books for all to read in the secret libraries.

I want our hearts and minds to unite and revolutionize. Don't want racism's fist to be super-sized.

And finally, I want every sacred word in every language – dead and alive – to be your first and last name. So whenever I call out to you, it feels like I'm praying.

MATTHEW BALDWIN

THE FORM WITHIN THE STONE

WANT TO BE ONE OF THE BEAUTIFUL PEOPLE. THE PROBLEM IS, I have no real idea what that actually means.

Accurately defining beauty is like trying to lift a bead of mercury with your bare hands. Certain things spring up when the word is tumbled around in my head, images and landscapes and people, but while I can tell you *what* about them I find beautiful, I cannot articulate *why*. Attempting to find a common thread other than my own subjective perception is an exercise in futility.

Being a writer, I retreat to my first refuge when confronted with a word I don't understand: the dictionary. Except the definition of beauty I find there is a perfect example of my conundrum: "The quality attributed to whatever pleases or satisfies the senses or the mind, as by line, color, form, texture, proportion, rhythmic motion, tone etc. or by behavior, attitude etc."

I'll give the dictionary credit for being accurate in its non-specificity, but really, that's it? Centuries' worth of effort by artists, poets, and philosophers and "whatever" is the best we can come up with? Is there really no quantifiable means by which beauty can be measured, other than the trite "eye of the beholder" aphorism?

The inclination here is to say, well, yes, of course there is. After all, the concept of a physical standard of beauty that exists as an attainable goal is pervasive in our culture, with entire industries based around it. Infotainment television programs and tabloid periodicals habitually rate the appearances of the current hot celebrities of the moment, dissecting their appearance down to the tiniest blemish. Beauty products are marketed with the underlying message that a woman's inherent genetic gifts simply aren't good enough.

A quick survey of the various men's and women's magazines commercially available is all it takes to spot the ubiquitous offers of self-improvement techniques they offer, especially since every headline for "Rock-hard abs!" or "Firm, tight buns!" is always coupled with some variant of "How to have your best sex ever!" The trend runs the gamut from *Playboy* to *Cosmopolitan*, *Men's Health* to *Women's Fitness*, each of which is gorged with images of nubile young things displaying miles of flawless skin and nonexistent reserves of body fat. They always seem happy! They probably have sex all the time! Who *wouldn't* want to look like them? And hey, if exercise and diet don't do the trick, a person can always turn to the array of chemical and surgical methods we've devised.

What this particular malformed subsection of our culture is really doing, though, is conflating *beauty* with *attractiveness*, which itself is just a coded term for sexual desirability. The equating of one with the other is, I think, a false and at times dangerous dichotomy. The thousands of eating disorders suffered by (mostly) women in the last few decades didn't develop spontaneously.

I won't deny that there's a relationship between the two, a tidal zone where they overlap and interact, but they are by no means synonymous; one is merely a function of the other. By merit of being a heterosexual male, my perspective of what is beautiful is in part shaped by my attraction to the female form, but it is not dictated by it. I recognize in my platonic female friends those same traits I would name as beautiful in a young woman I pass on the street – a stray tussock of auburn hair, perhaps, or the gentle curve of a calf muscle half hidden under the hem of a skirt – without the stirring of lust the latter provokes in me. And while I might find a piece of architecture or a particular painting beautiful, I don't want to sleep with it.

Who exactly set this standard, I wonder? Who decided that these body types – the swollen, artificial breasts, the oversized muscles, the hairless genitals and ageless faces – were the unilateral epitome of human beauty? The cynic in me is able to come to only one conclusion: those who stand to profit from selling it to us. They've turned a single, monolithic idea of beauty into a commodity, one so mercilessly conformist that Marilyn Monroe, a woman universally regarded as lovely in her day, would be considered chubby if she emerged on the scene now. And the consuming public snaps it up and asks for seconds.

I don't care much for cosmetic surgery, except in cases of medical necessity or to repair extant injuries; it's the eye-candy equivalent of high fructose corn syrup. The plasticized, Barbie doll image of the typical *Playboy* Playmate has never struck me as particularly beautiful, their bodies all seemingly pressed from the same mold and subsequently airbrushed to a further degree of artificiality. No, give me instead the face of a sleeping lover in the soft light of the early morning, her features free of makeup and her hair tousled.

There was a lovely young woman I knew back when I was a student, with whom I used to share a bit of a flirtation though nothing ever came of it, as she only ever had eyes for other men. One night at a house party when we were both a bit drunk, however, she took me aside and showed me her breasts. I saw for the first time a scar on one, thicker than my finger, running a jagged line from areola to sternum, and understood why she never wore tops that showed off her cleavage, despite being amply gifted in that regard. She asked me how hideous I thought it looked, and when I told her it was worth kissing, this woman, who never suffered from a lack of male attention, burst into tears.

Perhaps what is most beautiful to me, then, about the human body is the extreme range of variety provided by such an unremarkable morphology. No horns, no feathers, no striped fur, just a torso, four limbs, and a head, which can still form so many interesting and different combinations that imposing such an arbitrary standard is simply cruel. It's the imperfections, those deviations from the form that give us our uniqueness.

Those trite aphorisms, damnable though they may be, are correct. Whatever pleases the senses or mind is a matter of subjective individual perception, and perception is adjustable. After all, a competent photographer with the right lenses can turn an unremarkable subject into a wonder to behold. So while I may not be able to concretely define even my own exact perspective on beauty, I can say this much: It should be verbally and vigorously recognized, whatever form it takes.

But where, then, does that leave me and my own body image struggles? Leaving aside the matter of my physical health, what goal am I working toward when I exercise? After all, doubtless there are plenty who would find me beautiful or attractive regardless of the state of my waistline.

Ultimately, I think, it comes down again to subjectivity. About me finding an expression of my physical self that satisfies my mind.

I'm not sure when I decided I don't like my body, or even if I ever consciously did. It wasn't until I began to lose weight that I realized just how unhappy I'd been with the sight of myself. I was, in fact, rather depressed over the matter, a strange epiphany to come to as I'd never considered myself a person with "body issues." Other than a mild hatred for my frequently uncooperative hair, my looks were simply my looks, and that was that. To hell with anybody who thought otherwise, I told myself.

Now, three days a week, I rise before dawn and head off to the gym, where I spend thirty-five minutes on a powered elliptical cross-trainer, running through a program designed for maximum calorie burn; afterward, I throw myself at the weight machines, pushing, pulling, or lifting pieces of heavy metal at angles intended to strengthen and sculpt my muscles. By the end of my workout, I'm surfing high on a wave of endorphins even though my body is a sweaty, stinky, and soon-to-be-aching mess. Still, the results are plainly visible: I've lost about fifteen pounds in the last month.

I subject myself to this regimen in part out of concern for my physical health. The excess weight I'd been carrying exacerbated a recent joint injury, and according to my doctor dropping pounds will both expedite my recovery and prevent the injury from becoming chronic. But there's another reason, as well, one that caters to a level of vanity I'm ashamed to admit to.

Turns out that underneath this contrarian ambivalence was unhappiness buried so deep I'd forgotten it was there; it surfaced like an exhumed corpse once the initial results of my workout routine became evident. Discovering how happy I am with the newer version of myself taking shape meant confronting how much I disliked the old model, which I am only now able to confess. I wasn't simply heavy; I was genuinely overweight, and it was having profoundly negative effects on my physical and mental health, and had been for so long that I'd ceased noticing.

But where to go from here? I don't want to look like the people in those magazines, my appearance a product of plastic and chemicals. I've no desire for the bulgy muscles of a bodybuilder. But my early-morning workouts, at first such a chore to undertake, have become a joy. As I slim down, I sleep better, have more energy, and yes, am even feeling sexier and more attractive. I admit that I like this feeling, superficial though it may be, but not as much as I love the physical sensation of my body as this efficient, organic machine, one growing more and more refined with every stride on the elliptical or lift of the dumbbell. Regardless of what the final destination of my physique may be, I'm enjoying the journey.

In an art class I took in college, there was an anecdote passed around about the Renaissance artist Michelangelo. Michelangelo claimed he had no idea what the end result would be when he was presented with a fresh block of marble. He believed that there was already a work of art formed inside the stone, and it was only a matter of chipping away the excess around the statue until the next *Pietà* or *David* presented itself.

That sounds like a good enough plan to me.

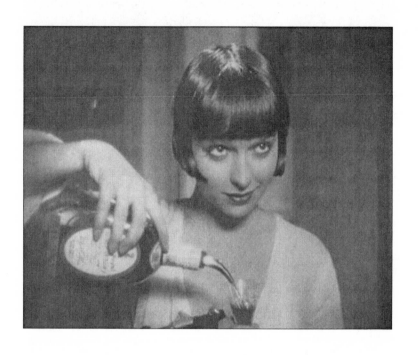

MELISSA FEBOS

CRAZY
BEAUTIFUL

RAGIC BEAUTY HAD ALWAYS BEEN THE SORT I ASPIRED TO. Tough, stumbling, hopeless hotness. I used to watch old Marlon Brando and Paul Newman movies and never quite knew if I wanted to save them, fuck them, or *be* them. That distinction was always a hard one for me. For a long time, it was exactly the sort of ambiguity I hoped to inspire.

In my disastrous, drug-addled late teens and early twenties, my beauty ideal accorded perfectly with my lifestyle. Convenient, though not coincidental. I saw myself as some kind of irresistibly hot, hopeless mess, the sort that promised a really good time for all the trouble.

The hijinks associated with so frequently being wasted I saw as a kind of bravery. I was very hardcore. Key points in my case for being a romantic antihero included the following list of things that happened on my dates:

- Loitering around pay phones for hours in sweltering August heat
- Nodding out in bars with an ice pack tied to my head
- Giving head to my girlfriend on the sidewalk of Avenue B
- Puking out of the window of my car, while driving
- Stubbing out cigarettes on my arm
- Pissing behind bushes, cars, in my purse, or in my pants
- Shooting up with toilet water in the bathroom of a Lower East Side bar without a functioning sink

Gross, yes. Stupid, yes. Antisocial, perfectly. But, according to my belief system around the turn of the century, gross, stupid, pathological traits could go from bad-crazy to good-crazy with the right leather jacket. I might crash your car, puke in your mouth, and cheat on you, but I made *really* good mix tapes, made eye contact when it mattered, and could charm your mom in a blackout. I was *good* crazy.

"You're *crazy!*" my dates would yell at me, their eyes shining with admiration. They were twenty, too, and none of us knew that running around acting crazy is usually just running away.

Fast forward ten years and a lot had changed. I got sober and replaced the drugs with more frequent showers, regular meals, and semi-appropriate clothing. Not only that, but after a few years without a drink or a drug in me, my belief system shifted along with my body's chemistry. After working on the inside of my head for a while, the outside of my life started looking not-so-bad.

My boyfriend (the only person I'd ever dated who had a steady job) and I had just bought a swanky new condo in a swiftly gentrifying Brooklyn neighborhood; I was teaching creative writing to college students, and I'd finally sold my first book—a memoir about my past experiences as a professional dominatrix and heroin addict and exactly how unlovely that time had become, in retrospect. Life was good. It sure wasn't what I'd wanted back in the late 1990s, but I had changed. I was a citizen now. I voted. I had long hair, a graduate degree, and a vitamin regimen. I was the opposite of my old self. I had everything I wanted, right?

I'd never been the kind of little girl who fantasized about diamond engagement rings, gleaming new-construction condos, or Kennedy-style afternoons on the patio with my WASPY in-laws. But then, I'd always rejected those clichés with the conviction of someone convinced she didn't qualify for them in the first place. I'd chosen ugly/pretty because it suited my politics, but also because pretty/pretty wasn't on the menu for me. In junior high school, I'd stopped shaving my armpits and pierced my own nose because I was a tiny feminist and I liked the way it looked. But I also knew I was too bookish and big-titted and vegetarian to ever be a cheerleader. I didn't read *Seventeen* magazine and go to football games; I made 'zines and had a secret eating disorder.

But after years of defining myself by choices made in defiance of social prescription, I was happily resigned to having sold out, or given in, or grown up, or let go, or because I'd simply fallen in love at a certain age, I discovered that I wasn't immune to the desire for diamonds, or babies, or Kennedy-style afternoons on my in-laws' patio—even if every Sunday I was sweating underneath long-sleeved cardigans that hid my tattoos and claiming that my forthcoming memoir was just about my "wild college years." I wasn't hiding; I just had less to prove, right? I felt good, mostly. I felt beautiful, mostly, and in a way I'd never thought I would.

But still, that instinct for extremity kept popping up in its relentless Whack-a-Mole-ish tenacity. After five years of total, continuous sobriety, I found myself:

• Standing around for hours in Central Park in the dead of winter
• Falling asleep in the afternoon with ice packs tied to my knees
• Running circles around Prospect Park in ninety-degree heat for so long that my tits bled and my toenails loosened like rotten teeth, turned black, and fell off

But that was just from my marathon training. Turns out, there are plenty of socially accepted forms of perverse extremity. You don't have to be a junkie, spank anyone, or get spanked for a living to experience the exhilarating numbness of pushing your human limits. This kind of extremity was arguably *healthy*, wasn't it? My sober running didn't qualify as running away from anything, the way my old running around had ... right?

I mean, I was happy. My boyfriend and I were in couples' therapy, making progress.

"I don't really like the book," he told me. "It's my least favorite thing you've ever written."

"I'd rather work out maniacally, or watch porn at my desk, than have sex with you," I thought, but didn't say.

Sure, he worked more hours than any human ought to, and there was that anger thing that once led him to smash an entire box of Tofutti Cuties against his forehead one by one.

This wasn't easy, but when had I ever chosen anything *easy*? Relationships weren't supposed to be easy. And also, it was the best

I'd ever done at loving someone. I was committed to not leaving, because that's what I wanted to learn how to do sober—*stay*. And we loved each other. I hadn't been able to let anything hold that much of me since heroin.

So why couldn't I stop thinking about my neighbor? Our courtship started the usual way—with a little Facebook stalking and some innocent texts that I deleted immediately. The trouble began in earnest when I rode on the back of her scooter to a reading that we never attended—instead trading stories of our criminal histories on a stoop. When I told her about getting banned from C-Town for doing whip-its and hiding the empty whipped cream cans in the dog food aisle, *in my twenties*, instead of exclaiming how she couldn't imagine such a thing, she laughed, and told me about when she accidentally set her bed on fire. So I laughed, and told her about when I accidentally set my bed on fire. After that night, the clump of feelings in my gut grew into a hernia and became harder to ignore.

I'd never been immune to crushes in relationships, but I hadn't ever acted on them sober. She was too much my type, too much of everything that didn't come with my new condo, and smelled way too good for me to let our "friendship" progress into the realm of mix tapes with neon subtexts. I knew her well enough already to know that I didn't have long before she blew the cover off our friendship—she was too honest not to say what we were both thinking.

One of the convenient things about those of us with a tendency for addiction is our preternatural ability to pretend that something is anything other than what it is. So long as we don't say it out loud. When she finally looked at me and said, "I don't want to be your stupid friend," I knew I was triple-fucked.

At the outset of that summer, I could see further into my future than I ever had before. September of 2009 showed that picture upturned: I had broken up with my boyfriend, was in post-breakup couples' therapy, desperately searching for a new place to live while camping out on my side of the now disarrayed condo, smoking cigarettes again, and, to my great surprise, falling in love. All while teaching seven college classes.

I had stopped running.

What happened in between is the exciting part—the three months I spent feeling like I was going to shit my pants, and having the best sex of my life. During those months I saw my knees hit the floor of more than one public restroom, not to puke, but to pray that I'd survive the way I felt. I felt the kind of crazy you can only know sober, feeling every breeze of self-loathing, every inch of becoming more myself, every glimpse of my anticipated future disintegrating. I couldn't even see into next week anymore.

Before every class I taught that fall semester, I stood outside my classroom door and took a deep, shaky breath, convinced that this time I wouldn't be able to pull it off. My voice would falter, and I would dissolve into a professorial puddle before my bright-eyed students, nothing left of their once-confident mentor but a crumpled, pearl-buttoned cardigan. It never happened. When I walked in, everything would simply fall away, leaving me, my students, and the small miracle of whatever story we were discussing. Slowly, I started to have a little more faith, and I stopped wearing pearl-buttoned cardigans.

A year later, I'm still teaching college, still going to bed on the early side, and back to running regularly. But now, I don't hide my tattoos from anyone. My fitness routine doesn't cause more damage to my body than benefit. I've put on ten pounds. I look a little bit less like everyone else, and a little bit more like myself. And my relationship? Well, it's pretty damn easy.

Here's the thing: Bodily pain is something to withstand. Risking your physical safety, or even your dignity—sure, maybe those are acts of bravery, or toughness, or simply self-disregard. Or maybe they are desperate attempts to avoid having to withstand that greater risk, of having an earnest feeling, of being *still* long enough to be seen, or to see how you've changed what you touch. In my experience, risking your ass is a lot easier than risking your heart. Being completely awake for every kiss, every choice, every fuck, every risk: That's the most hardcore beauty I have ever experienced.

MARNI GROSSMAN

PRETTY IS AS PRETTY DOES

My mother says that beauty is in the eye of the beholder. She says that beauty is only skin deep.

My mother says that I'm gorgeous. She says that I'm adorable. That I'm not fat, no, she swears, it's the truth. My mother says *I wish you could see yourself the way I see you.*

Right, I say with a smirk. *Through love cataracts.*

My mother says there will be days like this. There'll be days like this, my mother says.

We are one. An undulating mass of freshly shaven legs, glitter eye shadow, cheap taffeta, and hormones.

We are women. We are thirteen.

The Mighty Mighty Bosstones are playing. Or possibly Sugar Ray. "Bad Touch" or "Mambo No. 5."

When a slow song comes on, people pair up. Pair off. Mary Nash with Roger, Anna with Alex. No one comes for me, though, and "we" becomes "I." Alone, I stand around for a minute, nervously picking at my dress. But I'm not stupid, not blind. I beat a hasty retreat.

I walk fast, with purpose, to the bathroom. In the mirror I can see that I am not what I thought I was. Under the fancy dress, I'm just me. Ugly.

I lock myself in a bathroom stall and hang my head between my legs waiting for the moment to pass.

I am, in fact, intimate with ladies' rooms. With powder rooms and lounges, the loo, and the john. In fact, sometimes I feel as though my life has been nothing more than a long line of evenings spent hiding in bathroom stalls.

MY FACE IS THE SHTETL. I AM GALICIA. I AM THE WARSAW Ghetto. I am Zabar's. I am the new Woody Allen film. I am some tertiary Philip Roth character.

Because my eyes are dark and brown and heavily lidded, they are often described as soulful. Or mournful. Sorrowful. There's something of Susan Sontag in them. And there's a bit of Rosa Luxembourg in my long, hooked nose. Or maybe Emma Lazarus. In my smile, there are echoes of Anne Frank.

I invite comparisons—not to movie stars, but to Holocaust victims and Ellis Island rejects.

Even my body is foreign: fleshy and puckered. Tits and ass and hips. I have unruly brown pubic hair, one part Chia Pet, one part steel wool. I have a faint mustache that I bleach faithfully. My hair gets greasy and my skin is dotted with fading pimples. I am neither svelte nor toned. It's telling: There's no English word for *zaftig.*

I am much too much.

I AM NOT A PRETTY GIRL. I KNOW THIS, BUT, AT THE SAME TIME, I'm hoping someone will come along to contradict me.

I'm not a pretty girl and the most I can aspire to is "striking."

Striking. Or "unusual."

In college, a friend asked me to be in her student film. "You have such an *unusual* face," she said.

But everyone knows, of course, that "unusual" is the polite word for ugly.

PRETTY IS AS PRETTY DOES, THE SAYING GOES. BUT THE THING of it is, pretty does well.

Studies show that being attractive comes with plenty of benefits. Pretty people make more money, more friends. They get more sex and better jobs.

And while my mother would have me believe that beauty comes in all shapes and sizes, science says otherwise. Beautiful people, they say, have symmetrical faces. Lithe bodies. Wide-set eyes and generous mouths.

Even babies know this.

In 1989, psychologist Judith Langlois found that infants have an innate sense of what is and is not attractive and act accordingly. The babies in her study stared significantly longer at attractive faces than at unattractive ones.

Which is to say that I am, and always have been, doomed.

PRETTY IS AS PRETTY DOES, THE SAYING GOES. BUT WOMEN have always known this to be a fallacy. We know that all we've got is the curve of our ass. That a pretty face is worth more than a PhD. We know that when our looks fade, we will be irrelevant, obsolete.

We know this and so we spend our lives, our money, trying to be beautiful. We tweeze and we pluck and we shave and we wax. We curl our eyelashes and we host Botox parties. We starve ourselves or we corrode the pipes with our vomit. We go under the knife again and again. We buy, buy, buy.

And we never give up the hope, propagated by Hollywood and children's books, that we will wake up one day and be–quite suddenly–transformed. A swan.

FOR WOMEN, LOOKS MATTER. PRETTY IS PRETTY DAMN IMPOR-tant. I always knew this. And when I was sixteen, I decided that if I wasn't going to be beautiful, I'd better be thin. If I was thin enough, I reasoned, no one would notice that I was ugly. Models, after all, are allowed to be unusual. To have crooked noses that meander left-ward and asymmetrical faces. So I'd be thin. Yes.

Yes.

And for a while, I was. I was very thin. I was ninety-five pounds and then, for a moment, eighty-eight pounds.

But I was also starving. I was puking in the shower and cutting my stomach with razor blades. And I wasn't any prettier.

MY FRIEND LACEY RECENTLY TAGGED THIS AWFUL PHOTO OF ME on Facebook. I de-tagged it. Because I'm vain and I'm insecure.

"I look hideous," I wrote on her wall. "And fat."

In the picture, I'm in the midst of a story, in full flow, prattling on about something or other. I'm clasping my tote bag. Emily Martin's *The Woman in the Body* is poking out. Maybe I'm extolling its virtues.

My breasts look enormous, and so does my nose. I look heavy and cow-like and the photographer has, unflatteringly, shot me from below. Also, it's my bad side.

And so I de-tagged the picture. Of course I did.

The picture continued to haunt me, though. I couldn't get the image out of my mind. Ugly with a capital U. It wouldn't go away.

It wouldn't go away because, I think, it really did look like me.

This is what I look like, I told myself. Caught up in the moment. Living and breathing and reading and, yes, eating. *This is what I look like.* No careful cropping, no artful lighting. Just…candid. *This is what I look like.*

It may not be pretty, but it's the truth.

Nora Burkey

THE POLITICS OF BEAUTY

Whenever I show friends or family pictures of the female students I taught in Cambodia, they usually remark the same thing: They're all so *beautiful*.

What's strange to me is how this is the first thing I always hear, as if the reason poverty is unfair is because it means beautiful people don't have the chance to show the world just how beautiful they are.

As if it's unfair that beautiful people have to be poor.

As if it would somehow be okay if the world's ugly people were sent to the same poverty-stricken island to perish.

Next to the largest high school in Siem Reap, Cambodia—Angkor High School, educating about five thousand students daily—there is a dormitory for thirty girls from Cambodia's countryside. The dorm resembles a maximum security prison, down to the barbed wire lacing the top of the walls. Men are not allowed to enter the enclave, and there are no exceptions to this rule. Fathers squat outside the premises next to the girls' brothers and friends. All volunteers must be women, though the foundation that enables these poor girls to go to school is run by a Cambodian man named Paul, a wiry, excited, young tour guide equipped with an arsenal of English buzz words like "networking" and "empowerment." Years ago, Paul handpicked his crop of girls by conducting interviews, screening for "leadership potential." *Leader* is the role he wants to breed them for.

I first met the girls from this foundation at a TOMS shoes distribution. TOMS is the company that exploits Western consumerism by promising to send free canvas shoes to someone, somewhere, for each pair sold in the wealthier world. TOMS didn't show for the distribution but asked that the recipients take pictures of the event and send them back to the company, presumably to their marketing team. So, the poor Cambodian girls who'd been gifted TOMS shoes stood crowded around their school's green-tiled kitchen, a large space open to the outside with one sink and a few charcoal burners. Some girls posed for the camera with the best model's pose, others took the shoes off immediately after the photographs, complaining that the back of the shoe hurt. (Many people from Cambodia's countryside have never worn a shoe restricting their ankle. Even farmers wear flip-flops, or go barefoot.)

From the ankle up, the girls wore ripped jeans with Tweety Bird and Hello Kitty patched on the leg. Their shirts boasted sayings in the English language, such as *Princess* or *Sassy Girl*. Some girls wore shirts designed for men. But ankle down, they now had something different, something new. Incidentally, the girls needed new shoes for school. The principal had recently decided all students must wear "real" shoes, with backs that hide ankles and fronts that hide toes, because, the theory went, out in the "real" world, people wear "real" shoes. I couldn't help but feel that "real" was supposed to mean "better." Is it possible for one type of footwear to be categorically "better" than another? Shoes cannot be representative of rotten things, the way it is clear life under Stalin was worse than life under Franklin Delano Roosevelt. Shoes are not politics, are they?

Well, maybe. One girl from the dorm was able to wear only one shoe. Her left leg is atrophied and she uses a crutch to walk, so no shoe ever goes on this foot. A Cambodian woman affiliated with the foundation told the girl to go in the front of the photograph. "If she goes in the front," she told me, "everyone will feel sad and send more money to Cambodia. She must go in the front." I didn't know the best way to tell this woman I doubted very much there was any truth to her statement. If TOMS shoes were any proof, people give when they get something back. What could this girl possibly give back? She was so shy she could barely speak, so poor she couldn't afford the fifty cents that shoes cost in Cambodia.

The woman later instructed the girls to be grateful for their new shoes because the same pair cost $60 in America. I wanted to disappear, fearful that the only thing the girls would see when they looked at me was everything people in my country hold dear: fashion, getting noticed, looking right and desirable in a world of suffering.

Is it not politics when some people can spend $60 for their twentieth pair of shoes and still others cannot afford to attend school without the help of a foreign government or foreign donors?

And is it not political when outside parties decide what is best for the people of Cambodia, decide how to make their culture "better," decide that they're so far not good enough?

Months later, I was asked by an affiliated American woman to aid a computer class at the high-security dorm. When I arrived there for my second time, I spent one hour swiveling around on an office chair, watching as several Cambodian men worked on computers, the machines humming from hard work in the heat. Mosquitoes buzzed around us, though I was the only one who noticed or seemed bothered. The men were quiet and reserved. We all smiled at each other and asked for names, then forgot the answers. I looked at their résumés until Paul and his staff showed up. Each was typed in English. From what I read, the men apparently all enjoyed playing volleyball and practicing their English.

Half as many girls as boys attend school in Cambodia, and even fewer girls enroll in college to work with computers. In order to get computers installed in his dorms, Paul had to hire men. He and his staff of three American women agreed: The first priority was protecting their girls, which meant the several grown men in front of me needed a babysitter.

"We don't know what these men will do," one of the American women with short white hair told me. "They could go into their rooms and do something bad." Inside each bedroom there are at least ten bunk beds. For rapes to be successful, all nineteen witnesses would have to stand back and watch, not one running for help.

"That could happen?" I asked, unconvinced.

"Cambodian men don't act right around girls," she said, as if this were a *de facto* rule I had yet to hear about. But I wondered: If I were to assume that all Cambodian men were potential rapists, why exactly was I, a young woman, chosen for the role of supervisor? The answer came soon enough.

"You're a Western woman," Paul said. I noticed his fingernails were exceptionally groomed. "You're an independent woman. Girls in Cambodia are not like girls in your country."

He explained that Cambodian girls were shy and didn't want to speak their minds, that for this they needed an example. He wanted me to be their example, and also their computer-class helper.

"It is easy to teach them," he said, "because my girls are like blank pieces of paper. Anything you put on them will stick." He pushed his thumb against a white piece of paper to demonstrate.

He also wanted me to write reports on each man who was working with the computers and comment on what they were doing to the machines and classroom. I knew they were all at least five or ten years older than me, with an understanding of computers I wasn't even close to touching. I told him I didn't think I was the best person for the job, that we barely understood each other, and that I certainly didn't know what they were doing well enough to write about it. Even had they been able to explain in English, I was doubtful I would understand their technical terms.

"Don't worry," he said. "We need a Western woman. That makes our foundation look important. They think you're important."

An excellent message, I thought, for the empowerment of teenage girls in Cambodia. Nothing else matters but how you look to other people. White faces mean importance.

The liberation of women in developing countries is a hot topic in the political world. Cambodia—a country where girls are half as likely to be literate as boys are and "good" women come home before 6 P.M.—is certainly under scrutiny. I lose hope when a foundation dedicated to women's empowerment acts against progress.

I spent a total of four months in Cambodia, and never did I feel women were treated as lesser individuals more than when I met Paul and his team of three American women. Every time, their message left me wanting to run in the opposite direction.

One time Paul asked twenty-two-year-old Jenna (who lives in New York City off her father's money) to teach a feminism lecture. Jenna's qualifications were similar to mine: She was a Western woman. She spent two nights with the thirty girls in a hot, sticky classroom connected to their bedrooms. The classroom contained three broken fans, another thing only men could be hired to fix, and later *were* hired to fix (*these* men, however, were trusted by the Americans, as one was a priest).

Jenna said of the girls, "They don't have real body-image issues. They don't think they're fat or anything. They just want to be white." Only weight issues were "real," is what I gathered Jenna meant.

Her decision for their second class was to show them a picture of Beyoncé Knowles, "who is both dark and beautiful." I'd no idea qualified feminists thought that thin and rich Ms. Knowles was the epitome of "inner beauty" in the Western world. Of course, none of the girls understood a word Jenna spoke to them. She lectured them in English, in which their skills are severely limited.

Even if they had understood her, a few hours of Feminism 101 does not quite take down the competition. Billboards dot the city: "Be white," they all say.

Some men in Cambodia wear makeup to lighten their faces, and most soap contains a whitening agent.

Before I arrived in Cambodia, I knew it to be a country that stands not quite on its own two feet. It is a country with one of the largest NGO presences in the world. Until I arrived, I didn't know that each NGO delivers its own brand of liberation. What exactly were these girls being taught? That as females they had the *right* to be beautiful, the *right* to be protected from the men of their society, who are unscrupulous in whom they take for sexual prisoner? Should a feminist believe that all men rape? That skinny, rich, and famous dark women from America are at the forefront of feminism? That all Western women are liberated?

In country, the beliefs were a little different. One conviction I encountered many times was a conservative one, a "pull yourself up" mentality about how poverty doesn't mean you have to be unclean.

The lack of food and access to school and beauty products in Cambodia was old news. At the dormitory, a different American woman, this one younger and agreeable to everything Paul said, asked if I'd be willing to show the girls how to wash their hands better. She said this is something they often neglected because they really didn't know how. Their "backward" parents had never taught them. She also complained of them not wearing deodorant. They were teenagers, after all, and should have been concerned about the smell of their underarms.

I declined her offer. It was not the students' duty to be beautiful like me, clean like me. Was it fair to ask them to be cleaner when they showered with a cold hose they shared with twenty-nine others and lived off ten dollars of spending money a month? Thirty teenage girls with no toilet paper or tampons, who would do anything for the chance to go to school, could keep their hands dirty if they wanted, I thought. Who was I to call this backward? Time doesn't go that way.

This is politics to me: when a wise, old Cambodian woman asks me why white people are so clean and Cambodians are so dirty.

It is politics to me when a belief such as this penetrates a civilization and makes people feel lesser.

It is politics to me when I see that cost-of-living discrepancies are somewhat of a myth, when I see that a bottle of Pantene Pro-V shampoo costs $4.25, or about four to five days' worth of food for the average Cambodian living in Siem Reap. It is politics when I see that the only cheap shampoos have whitening agents in them, when even the cheapest products cost too much for people who live on less than a dollar a day. Over half the people in Siem Reap province live below the poverty line. Almost all houses and stores have no doors or window screens, just openings dust and dirt can easily fly through.

Are Cambodian people dirty, as the older women suggested, or do they, as I think, merely live outside, in houses constructed with minimally processed materials such as sticks and straw?

According to Betsy, a woman from England I met during my stay, the people of Cambodia don't know the meaning of being clean. Betsy started a hygiene program in a rural school next to Cambodia's landmine museum, claiming it was high time that children learn to take off the dirt that is "tattooed on them."

Betsy, according to her friends, "has more money than God," but she didn't ask any Cambodians whether a hand-washing station at a rural school would be a desirable use of her money. She didn't ask the teachers or the principal where they'd like to see cash spent. Rather, she hired Cambodian men to install a sink and then yelled at them in English for doing it wrong, telling them they were using no logic, although her knowledge of plumbing amounts to zero. The sink went near the bathrooms, near latrine holes in the ground that are flushed with a small bucket of water.

What makes a person beautiful and right looking? Does it require wealth, or an English benefactor who installs sinks? If it had been only their access to soap Betsy worried about, I might have saluted her efforts. Hand-washing reduces disease, and washing one's hands after using a bathroom with no toilet paper is a good idea. But it wasn't only their health Betsy worried about; it was their brains.

Her case in point: Most brooms are only hip-length tall in the region. One day, when the children were cleaning the classrooms (something they and the teachers do every week, as "janitors" are unaffordable), she grabbed a hip-length broom from a student's hand and gave him what she called a "proper broom," the pole handle of which reached to the shoulder. The floor was not any cleaner for it.

"No logic at all," she repeated, and called Cambodian people stupid. How could they possibly think a hip-length broom would do the trick?

This is politics to me: when a wealthy woman from far away can tell a child the systems of his country are stupid and useless. Cambodians don't use ovens to cook. Is this incorrect, too?

I don't understand what drives these people. What drives Paul to make leaders out of girls he considers impressionable blank pieces of paper? What drives Jenna to de-legitimize skin color as a real body-image issue? What drives some American women to consider all Cambodian men would-be rapists? What drives Betsy to make an "illogical" country cleaner?

Was it innate stupidity that made my sixth-grade students present me with these gifts for Christmas: two toothbrushes, two tubes of toothpaste, three individual-use packets of shampoo, two bars of soap, and many rubber bands to hold my hair back? Was it true that they don't know the meaning of being clean, as Betsy would say? Or is it true that they cherish cleanliness because it is unaffordable to them? Did they gift me these things because they thought Western people valued cleanliness above all, and they wanted to give me something special to me and my culture, rather than special to them and their culture?

If the tables were turned, if Cambodians came to America or England to help, would they arrive with ancient pots and pans, toss the plug-in rice cookers from everyone's homes, and hack the doors from the walls to make life look proper again? Thanks to politics, and a global economy, we don't have to imagine such a scenario. But I know where I stand on the question.

Where is the real beauty to be found in Cambodia? Is it in being white and clean? Is it in starving kids with distended bellies who are finally able to hold their pencils with scrubbed, clean hands? Or that there are small children in this world with dirty faces and fingernails who, as they walk through rice fields and look after their cows, wonder how best to say thank you to their teacher?

Rice paddies require floods of fresh water, and yet the people who work them become wet and dirty, the roads to their fields often a quicksand of animal dung.

What is it that the Cambodians cherish? Would it have been better for Betsy to give the Cambodians something they held dear? Or does she figure that if people scrub hard enough, they can wash off their brown color, or wash money into their pores, making Cambodia a better, richer country? A more Western place to live?

I will never forget some sentences my student Tida wrote in her notebook. She wrote, "My teacher is prettier than me," and "My teacher is smarter than me." I told her that she was wrong, so she erased both sentences and tried again, believing I was scolding her for incorrect English form. Tida was eleven years old and looked to be only seven, her growth stunted long before I'd met her. Her clothes were always unclean, her legs filthy, and I found her remarkably beautiful. For her appearance, yes, as all people I care about look beautiful to me, but also for her gifts and notes of thanks, her concern about making sure I had a good Christmas because I was so far away from home.

Days before I left the country, I gave Tida and the other girls in my class small hairbrushes with mirrors. I gave the boys the Cambodian version of hacky sack, called a *sei*. The girls were jealous of the boys, and it was then I realized how wrong everyone had been about Cambodian girls, about what they needed and what they wanted.

The next day, I brought all the girls a *sei*, and a chance to play with the boys. I saw that they didn't want to be beautiful or clean, like me. Tida may have believed that I was "beautiful," that "beauty" in the physical sense was important to me, but I knew that she didn't envy me my differences. She was Cambodian and comfortable that way, with a little dirt on her legs and arms, with messy hair.

I wish I had given more to the people of Cambodia. I taught English lessons; I helped two homeless high school girls find a home; I bought a volleyball for the boys and girls at a nearby orphanage. I wish I had given more, but I'm proud at least of what I gave the girls at the dorm: the right to be dirty, the right to be like men, the non-raping kind.

Near the river that runs through Siem Reap, there are several volleyball courts where men play shirtless. We arrived with my friend Denny, who bought a court for us and coached the girls through their first public game. Soon everybody was watching us, *the bad women.*

Good women stay at home. Good women don't play sports. Good women remain clean. Is it possible that there is a younger generation of Cambodian men who aren't buying it, either?

Who wants liberation for the women of their country as badly as the women want it? Who wants to give their sisters and their wives the chance to have choice? Perhaps the seeds of change are hard to see from a Western eye because so often liberated women look like our women. Liberated women look like me and wear shorts above the knee as if clothes were the meaning of independence.

Does liberation have to be politically motivated? Does it have to look the same across two distinctly different cultures? Does cleanliness make a good woman, a better person, a freer country?

Later that week, Denny took the girls fishing with his brothers, just opposite the volleyball courts. The girls wrapped a heavy, wet fishing net around their arms and let it fly, pulling it back to shore along with several tiny silver sea creatures. They all returned home filthy and smelling of fish, wearing long pants as is expected in Cambodia. Smiles were painted on all of their faces.

"They're never allowed outside," Denny told me. Together, he and I broke the rules, and it had nothing to do with the way anyone dressed.

In the end, I guess I was a good leadership example, despite defying Paul's regulations. I hope the girls saw me the way they saw themselves. Like them, I wore no makeup or jewelry. I ate at local places, lived with a local family, and accepted the impossibility of remaining clean in Cambodia, even in the cool season. You'll drip with sweat every minute and, unless encased in plastic (as every product from every store is) you'll be covered in dust from the red dirt paths.

Life in Cambodia exists outside. I suggested to the older woman who complained of a dirty kitchen that it wasn't necessarily dirty; it was merely *outside*.

If you want to live a full life, sometimes you have to go outside and get dirt between your toes. And life should be beautiful – beautiful and ultimately free, meaning that in a perfect world, Cambodians would get to decide for themselves what is right, what is clean, what is beautiful, and what is feminism.

In a perfect world, Paul and Betsy would remain their own keepers, and no one else's. Of course, we don't live in a perfect world. We live in a political one, rife with food shortages and honor killings and "leaders" who want to maintain power over a world of suffering. So suddenly, looks, fashion, and hand-washing all seem to fall in importance, don't they?

To survive, we must find other kinds of beauty, to take our minds off all the darkness.

RACHEL POLLON

CHANGE FOR A TEN

His name was John. Not actually. But in an effort to protect the innocent—could be him, could be me—that's what we'll call him. So his name was John, and I met him when, let's say, I was eighteen and he was nineteen. I was working at a record store that might have been in the San Fernando Valley. He worked at a vintage clothing store just down the block. We were young, and we met, and we fell for each other.

He was the most beautiful boy I'd ever dated. Beautiful boys weren't necessarily my thing. I mostly went for rough ones. Ones I couldn't quite get to. Who seemed like something was wrong and that if I did just the right thing maybe they'd become happy and could love me the way I yearned to be loved. Wholly. I found them beautiful in their own way. Sadness, theirs and mine, seemed like beauty to me then.

But John was different. He was actually physically beautiful. Reminiscent of Gael García Bernal. He was also sweet, thoughtful, and present. He paid attention. For some reason, he liked me.

I was reminiscent of myself, and maybe early Molly Ringwald. Some people surely thought I was pretty, or cute, but I didn't. I didn't feel very pretty on the outside or the inside. But I had recently found a place where I felt right. At the record store. School wasn't speaking to me and I thought I wanted to be out in the working world. After one year of junior college, I followed my love of music east on Ventura Boulevard and got to be surrounded by it.

I'll be honest: I don't remember our first encounter. I wasn't shot in the heart and birds didn't suddenly appear. It was probably something along the lines of my working an evening shift and needing change for the cash register. Maybe I went down the block to his place of work to see if they could spare a roll of quarters in exchange for a ten. Some of us at the record store knew some of the people that worked at the vintage store. We were of the same ilk: Uncomfortable misfits who liked music and dressing unconventionally. We were, at our core, "un."

John and I started dating. He probably came to the record store and asked me out. He wasn't one of those annoyingly vague sorts. He'd let you know he was interested, and sweetly took you in his hand and led you along with him. He was romantic and passionate and light. He could kiss. Not sloppily. Attentively. We kissed for long stretches of time. He looked unflinchingly into my eyes.

Soon after we started dating, I got sick. Some kind of head-cold sick. Runny nose, pinhole-size pupils cushioned by red baggy eyelids sick. Pretty.

I stayed home from work and holed up in my house. I still lived at home with my father and younger brother. My father was around-ish. Like me, he also worked, and since he was in between wives and not tied down to anyone, he had a social life. So I was left to my own devices, but I wasn't entirely alone.

Anyway, after a day or two of being sick and at home, a cold sore appeared on my lip. Violent and humongous, with topography very similar to that of the city of Los Angeles. If one looked closely enough, and I'll admit not many did, so I've no one to corroborate, I swear you could see palm trees and a trail of cars on what seemed to be the 405. The cold sore planted itself in the corner of my mouth, which, in the ensuing days, started to crack and bleed whenever I laughed or smiled or ate or breathed.

John and I spoke on the phone multiple times a day. He'd check in during his lunch break and when he got home at night. John had a different living situation than I. He lived with an older gay man we'll call Lewis. Lewis was probably in his early thirties, a clothing stylist, and it didn't take long for me to realize that Lewis wanted John. It didn't take me long because Lewis was blatant about it. He was somewhat hostile to me and stated openly to both John and me, together and on our own, that he thought he could turn him. John laughed it off. They met and became roommates when John got a job interning at the clothing company Lewis styled for. John grew up with a single mother and some sisters and making clothes was something he was evidently bred to do.

When it became clear that my virus wasn't going anywhere soon, John said he missed me and wanted to visit. I told him how awful I felt and how awful I looked. If I'm not mistaken my period was also due. I was the whole package. He insisted none of it mattered and that he knew just the thing to get me feeling more optimistic. He inquired as to whether I'd ever seen the movie *Swing Time*. I had not. He said it was a film his family would watch over and over, a classic and a surefire mood elevator. *Mask* might have been more appropriate, given my current state, but with my body's defenses down I was no match for John's enthusiasm. I asked if he was sure he thought he could take it – my heinousness. He was sure. And so I relented.

He came over that night with the movie. When I opened the door he pulled me close, and I sank into his chest. When I looked up at him he said, "Your eyes look even bluer when you're sick." He sat next to me on the couch and I rested my head on his shoulder, partially watching Fred glide with Ginger across the dance floor, but mostly thinking about how lucky I was to have such a nice guy want to be with me. A guy who didn't flinch one iota when he saw me. Who emitted only joyfulness at being in my presence. Mr. Astaire jumped from a table to a chair, landed just out of reach from Ginger, then held his hand out for her to grab it. John mimicked the last part of the gesture from his sitting position and I reached out to hold on.

Eventually, I got better and my "Aqualung"-like state became a distant memory. A faint redness in the corner of my mouth persisted for a while but it wasn't anything some matte white powder and dark red lipstick, my look at the time, couldn't disguise. John and I were now a month or so into our relationship. Because of our living situations we didn't have a ton of privacy. Coupled with my weeklong sickness (plus healing time for the cold sore), and my not actually stated but more kept in mind and sometimes up for discussion "wait three weeks" rule, we had yet to find the time or place to "do it." I'd stayed late at his apartment a time or two, but Lewis was there, lurking, possibly setting fire to a crude doll made from strands of my hair, and thus, circumstances were somewhat tricky to maneuver.

This one night, however, we knew Lewis was going to be out at some event for a while and that we would have some time to ourselves. We'd both worked until about nine o'clock and by the time we got to his apartment we were ready to be with each other, to push everything else that wasn't us out of the way and just be. I remember that John's room was dark, with the exception of the light coming in from outside. His apartment unit was on the ground floor so when we were lying down the street light hovered just above and next to us like a bedside lamp. He was so handsome. Under fluorescent or natural light, a pleasure to gaze at. As we held each other, becoming ready for our next step, John told me he had to tell me something. He seemed to be steeling himself while also becoming softer. He looked at me square in the eye and said, "I have a pretty small penis."

I thought for a moment before speaking. "Come on," I probably said. "Don't worry about that."

But he insisted.

You may be wondering at this point how I might not have had an inkling about this up until now. How we could kiss and spend late nights together but for me not to have known anything might have been … out of sorts. As mentioned, I had that rule, so the first week or so I was probably trying not to tease him. Then I got sick and all cold sorey. And then we're back into the story. I may have brushed my hand across the front of his pant leg a time or two but I probably thought I was feeling the zipper area. Or that he was favoring the other side that I wasn't pawing at. I was young. And perhaps blinded by his kindness and beauty.

So then I probably told him just to kiss me.

And we kissed and we touched and we eventually were undressed and then I touched it and then I saw it. It was small. It was the size of maybe a seven-year-old's penis. It was the size of a pig in a blanket. I felt bad for it. But more because it looked like it needed caring for, not because I was so experienced and thought I wanted or needed a big fat penis to be satisfied. I honestly hadn't dealt with that many penises up until that point, though the ones I did were lovely and nice. But I hadn't yet had the kind of sex that made me think, "Oh, that's why people do it." And I wouldn't with John, either.

We tried to have sex. Or rather, we did have sex, though I couldn't really feel anything. I felt his pelvic area against mine and I felt his lips on mine and his hands in my hair, but I didn't feel a penis inside of me. He asked how it was. I told him it was great, and we fell asleep there together with the street lamp shining its light of recognition upon us till dawn.

That morning when we got up and it was time for me to get home to shower and change before work, we crossed paths with Lewis in the kitchen. He was clearly bothered that I'd gotten to the finish line before he could, but he covered it with an overwrought account about the extraordinary night he had and how much John would have enjoyed it. It was probably a blessing. We didn't have to deal with our newest development. As I stood there awkwardly sipping a cup of coffee and taking on a supporting role while this scene unfolded, I noticed that John looked more vulnerable. Like he was seeing everything through my eyes.

John and I lasted for a few more weeks after our night. We went out and had mindless fun. Saw bands and movies. We went through the motions of having sex a couple more times, but eventually the intensity of what we had dwindled. It wasn't because of any sort of conscious disappointment on my part, and it wasn't about the penis per se. It just felt like there wasn't anywhere else for us to go. Something was both missing and haunting us. What was promised now seemed to be a closed door.

I thought about John over the years for this reason or that—when I'd see a Gael García Bernal movie, for instance, or find myself at a kitschy party where mini hot dogs were served. I wondered if he ever found a way to make an intimate relationship work. I hoped that his situation wasn't a lifelong frustration. And that maybe there was such a thing as a mid-twenties puberty spurt.

Ultimately, it would seem we each possess our own version of a small penis. Our particular something that would make life easier if we could just overcome it. Fear, self-doubt, viral infections that blister…bad taste in music. All of us wandering about in this life together, trying to get by, hoping someone will see past what we know is less than ideal and be there to make us feel beautiful, make us feel fine, when we can't for ourselves.

James D. Irwin

FROM *THE VENUS DE MILO* TO PORNO MAGS: THE EVOLUTION OF BEAUTY, & VICE VERSA

Beauty is a strange and incredibly powerful thing. In Ancient Greece, Helen of Troy was so beautiful as to launch a thousand ships—not in the way we launch ships these days. She was not smashed against the hull in the way the Queen smashes bottles of champagne against our warships. It was more of a symbolic thing. A thousand ships went to war for her because, although times and cultures may vary, men have always and will always do anything to impress an attractive woman.

It's hard to imagine someone being *that* beautiful. In the 2004 film *Troy*, that's exactly what film producers had to do. The woman they chose was Freddie's sister, Diane Kruger. Diane Kruger is undoubtedly a very beautiful woman. Maybe not quite beautiful enough to launch a thousand ships, but certainly beautiful enough to listlessly masturbate over on a wet Sunday afternoon.

But beauty is also a concept open to incredible subjectivity. This is perhaps best exemplified by the vast amount of varying categories and subgenres in pornography.

Notions of what beauty is vary through time and throughout cultures. The fat chicks that we find repulsive and boner wilting used to be quite the opposite. Fat-bottomed girls really used to make the rockin' world go round. Some guys really like Asian girls. Others, in a room with the cast of *Charlie's Angles 2: Full Throttle,* would ignore Lucy Liu in favor of skinny white girl Cameron Diaz, or the fuller-breasted Drew Barrymore. While it would be slightly cruel to ignore Miss Liu, and while it may be ethically wrong to offer girls up as pieces of meat, you get the point. Everybody has a different idea of what they find attractive and what they don't, and it varies between cultures and it varies through time.

For example, we know that the average height of mankind has risen through history. We know this because of old buildings. I live in Winchester, which was a capital city in Roman time, and although little remains of Roman civilization there are many buildings from as far back as the seventeenth century. My favorite pub, The Wykeham Arms, has been standing since 1755. Other pubs I don't like as much are older, and the door frames are ridiculously low. I'm a little over 5' 7". I am not very tall and even I have to limbo under the door it's so low.

We would likely find women from those days freakishly short, while they would find a supermodel like Claudia Schiffer freakishly tall. We're simply predisposed to find "normal" attractive – that is to say, what our culture, our society, considers normal. That's why, on average, people of average height are considered more attractive than the more abnormally sized midget, or the 6' 6" skinny hipster. Of course, there are deviations from the norm. I, for example, find shorter girls more attractive, but then that can also be attributed to science – the genetic, primitive instinct to want to protect and so on.

The point I'm trying to make, I think, is that as beautiful as the ancient Greeks might have considered Helen of Troy, we wouldn't necessarily share the same opinion. We probably wouldn't. I mean I could be wrong; she could be five different kinds of beautiful our minds couldn't possibly imagine or comprehend. But there's a pretty good chance she was a really short Greek chick a bit hotter than average. I can't make any guarantee...well, except the guarantee that Helen of Troy was not a leggy blonde like Diane Kruger.

Of course there are differences in opinion in our modern times and cultures. As far as I'm concerned, Diane Kruger is stunningly beautiful and, to put it as crudely as possible, I would tap that. But not everyone would agree with me. A Chinese peasant farmer, for example, would probably find her face to be pale and alien; bearing in mind that we are scientifically predisposed to finding our cultural concepts of normality attractive, then "pale and alien" would be strange and unattractive qualities. Even within our own Western culture there would be differences of opinion. Some guys find darker skin more attractive; some of us are crazy about redheads; some people are plain racist, and a few people I know would be turned off by the fact that Diane Kruger is German. (We call these people racists, too.) Everyone is different; everyone has different perceptions of the world and of beauty. Hell, some guys find other guys attractive. We're all different, and no one is right and no one is wrong.

That doesn't really stop anyone from fundamentalist Christians through to militant atheists from trying to argue otherwise, though. I mean, Jesus—how much longer can we argue about creation? Arguing over our creation—the creation of the world, the creation of the solar system and the galaxy and all of time and space…

Fuck it, can't we just sit back and appreciate the beauty within it all? Who cares who put it here, be it an omnipotent being, a flying bowl of pasta, or a bastard of an explosion? While we're all arguing about it, it's all passing us by. We could argue forever, but guess what? None of us will live long enough to do that.

The beauty of nature, of our planet and our star system and our infinite smallness in it, is as close to a universal appreciation as we can get.

It takes around twelve hours to cross the globe on a plane. No planet orbits closer to Earth than Venus, a beautiful gaseous purple orb, and we can only just make it out in our sky without powerful telescopic equipment. Mankind cannot travel to Mars, a distance so small in the relativity of space that it doesn't technically exist. There are four or five planets after Mars, depending on your feelings about Pluto, and that's just one solar system in one galaxy.

There is such beauty in the miniscule dimensions of space we can see: shooting stars, the tranquil seas of the moon, supernovas and stars, so many stars—orbs of burning fire that we see only as dim fairy lights across the inky canvas of the sky.

And there is nothing in space that can't be matched on our own planet. Picture the desolate deserts, the plunging oceans, home to strange and fantastical creatures. Imagine the twisting, snaking rivers of the Amazon, the Colorado, the Nile, and the Ganges and even the little babbling brook, the Itchen river that trickles serenely past my sixth favorite pub in Winchester. (Ah, Winchester, surrounded by rolling green hills that lack the power and impact of Ayers Rock or the Grand Canyon but have a small and quaint beauty of their own.) Then there are Norwegian fjords and gargantuan mountain ranges from Nepal to the Alps to the Rockies. There are the Giant Redwoods in California, sun-soaked beaches in the south of France or even Bondi beach. Also consider the fairy-tale snowfall and apocalyptic blizzards of Russia, or the unblemished snow of the North and South Poles.

There's so much beauty to admire and appreciate, and all we do as a species is argue about who put it here, and destroy large chunks of it because the people who live there have a different opinion on the matter—as though being right or wrong about the unanswerable question of existence is more important than existence itself.

The most ridiculous thing is that every major religion teaches peace, love, and understanding. There isn't an awful lot in those religious texts referring to smart bombs and terrorist sleeper cells. It's mostly love and kindness, two of the most beautiful acts a human being is capable of carrying out, forsaken for the most violent and selfish acts of which a man is capable.

Religion, like time, money, and pyramid selling, is a man-made concept. I'm no expert on theology, but I doubt that if there is a God he'd want us to argue like nuclear-armed school children over whether God is black, white, Arab, largely composed of spaghetti, or if he even exists at all.

It's like getting the greatest Christmas present you could ever think of—no, better than you could ever possibly imagine—and then spending the whole holiday arguing with your parents over who got it for you before getting bored of it and throwing it in a cupboard to slowly rot or rust or disintegrate.

Man is capable of creating beauty: Consider Beethoven's Ninth, the Sistine Chapel, Shane Warne's first delivery in international test cricket, St. Patrick's Cathedral, the Golden Gate Bridge, *Led Zeppelin III*, intricate computer systems that are ever more powerful and ever smaller, clockwork, Hamlet's speech in Act 11, Scene 1, and so much more.

And man is capable of appreciating physical, cosmetic, subjective beauty, from Helen of Troy to Grace Kelly, from Brigitte Bardot to Halle Berry, from Marilyn Monroe to Scarlett Johansson, from *The Venus de Milo* to Rubenesque portraits to good old twentieth-century porno mags.

And we *are* capable of appreciating beauty, and enjoying it in its purest forms free of social and territorial context, and free from religious divisions. Or maybe we will be someday. Maybe we'll step away from our Twitter feeds and smart bombs and appreciate our planet together, as one, before we annihilate it truly and completely.

Wouldn't that—all humanity together appreciating our existence as one, together—wouldn't *that* be beautiful?

Tyler Stoddard Smith

TRUTH AND BOOTY

People are always going on about beauty. But what, precisely, defines it? Ugliness is much easier and more satisfying to talk about. Hell, with the whole world gone pear-shaped, what is there to discuss but revulsion? Root canals, colonoscopies, my ex-wife. Is there any room for beauty anymore? Is the discussion relevant, even?

Well, when it comes to matters of beauty, as with judgments about Guinea worm disease or cyclic vomiting syndrome (although curiously not my ex-wife), the consensus has historically been that we should defer to the experts. Why not start, then, with the man who wrote of the "transcendental aesthetic?"

No wonder people have been flummoxed by the subject of beauty for the last 200+ years. In 1790, Immanuel Kant claimed that standards of beauty are like empirical judgments: They are valid across time and space. The old mandarin also said that an *inner* response provides the foundation for standards of beauty.

What were we *thinking*, taking beauty lessons from a seventy-three-year-old Teutonic virgin? Although a seminal advice column co-authored by Hegel and Kant in German *Vogue* (one has to make ends meet, even as a tenured philosopher) has been a veritable Rosetta Stone of beauty tips: "Entice your guy with a tropical-smelling unguent! Crack open a fresh coconut, and pour the milk into a *kleine Schüssel*. Add a scoop of gruel, and whisk it into a sexy froth. Spread it between your palms, and massage it over your body for an erotic treat—he will enjoy watching you do this, we think."

In the art department, Botticelli's ginger-haired *Venus* serves as a paragon of beauty, not only because the painting is old but also because *Venus* is mostly nude. Some philistines insist that *Venus* is "a little thick, needs a tan, and looks like a crazy Irish bitch I used to mess with. It's fine, though, how she can cover her pubes with her head hair." That's my roommate, Clint, who lacks a certain *je ne sais quoi*, but I do think the core of the problem lies in our misguided efforts to define beauty.

What follows are some thought-provoking (though often far-fetched) quotations by famous people on beauty, because what do *I* know about the subject?

KHALIL GIBRAN: *"Beauty is not in the face; beauty is a light in the heart."*
You can always count on inspirational claptrap of this sort from an undersexed Ottoman. From what I gather, the alleged "light in

the heart" is a reference to the sinoatrial node, which produces small electrical impulses that our celibate prophet confuses with light. Did Gibran have possession of the hexaxial reference system? No, because he's dead, and even if he weren't, you can't just go to the 5 & 10 store and find a quality ECG that will administer accurate lead placement. However, the first part of his statement has the ring of truth. Indeed, beauty is not in the face; it is *on* the face, like a cute little pug nose, a nice smile, straight teeth, maybe some long eye-lashes. You'll know it when you see it.

Maybe Gibran meant for his statement on beauty to be an alle-gory? I hope not. We, in today's world, take our symbols literally, so more than just confusing us, Gibran could be encouraging beauty seekers to carve each other open in search of ethereal "light," which is really just 70 MHz of current pulsing through a sea of brackish, cardiac soup. If you want light, hook up some nodes to a potato. If you're looking for beauty, stay away from Gibran's misinformed postulate(s) and check out those *cheekbones*. But beware! There's nothing like a tug on the heart strings, or fibrins (important proteins involved in platelet activation), to hoodwink the eye of the beholder.

RALPH WALDO EMERSON: *"Though we travel the world over to find the beautiful, we must carry it with us or we find it not."*

An ironic statement from a man who spent most of his life cooped up in his study, groaning about the "infinitude of the pri-vate man." To be fair, Emerson paid regular visits to Henry David Thoreau's yurt-cum-wattle house in Concord, and he once traveled to England where he confused Samuel Taylor Coleridge's opium for cinnamon (in the ensuing vision quest, he suggested Coleridge publish "Kublai Khan" as a "pop-up book," throwing Coleridge into a frenzy, who then asked the blitzkrieged Brahmin, "Why am I not getting any fucking buzz from this? This is exactly what you get when you deal with the Moroccans, Ralphie!")

So, Emerson's aphorism, in addition to having the linguistic typology of a nineteenth-century Yoda, becomes even more preposterous when you imagine folks traveling the world in search of a beauty they're already carrying. This is exactly the kind of un-Jedi assumption that would drive Yoda bonkers. To me, it reeks of greed. You just *said* you already had beauty somewhere on your person.

We do, however, travel the world in search of the beautiful, so why didn't the author just stop there? I'll tell you why: His life was devoid of beauty. Behind Emerson's back, and indeed, in front of his front, people often referred to him and his wife, Lydia, as "Dingo Fingers and The Manatee." And while verbosity on any subject may eventually carry the day, in the end, it's really just existential deception. You want beauty? There's a flight from LaGuardia to Miami Beach, $199 on Orbitz. If you find some beauty, it'll most likely be at The Bottoms Up Lounge on 8th Street, but my advice is not to carry it with you. If you do, I recommend a topical solution of Dynami-clear, two to four drops on the affected area.

PABLO PICASSO: *"Beauty? To me, it is a word without sense because I do not know where its meaning comes from nor where it leads to."*

One assumes a painter would appreciate the nature of beauty. Of course, Picasso uttered this cryptic line later in life, after gravity had taken its toll on his breasts, his head had become extraordinarily bald, and he had resorted to the last refuge of artists: the beret. Since the word "beauty" is, by his own admission, lost on him, we're forced to make sense of it ourselves, in the same way we make sense out of much of Picasso's art, especially his Athlete's Foot Period.

"Beauty... is a word without sense," he says. Sounds like somebody's got rocks in his *cabeza*. The ability to sense anything is, in and of itself, a thing of beauty. Take Christmas Eve. When you're seven, you can *sense* that Santa Claus is coming and you're going to get all the great stuff you asked for in the catalog, and it's almost better than the Tonka truck you don't get because Dad "sensed" that Tonka trucks were only for "Presbyterians." None of it makes sense, actually: On my seventh birthday, he sent me to a steeplejack camp for Satanists, and *last year* I got a Tonka truck.

Oh, I almost forgot! Where does beauty lead? To *getting your own apartment*—you're fucking thirty-two, Tyler. Shit.

GABRIELA MISTRAL: *"Beauty... is the shadow of God on the universe."*

You can always count on a Latina to come up with something esoteric and groovy when a simple explanation will do. Mistral, a Nobel Laureate, poet, autodidact, and amateur astronomer, became convinced that she had discovered beauty, that it was "the shadow of God on the universe." Well, a Nobel Prize in Lit does not a Galileo make, no disrespect. What theodicies were pin-balling around in that Chilean brain of hers? It's a nice little image, I grant you. But it's such an easy way out.

See if you can guess what went wrong with Gabriela Mistral's premature declaration about the nature of beauty:

With the plastic lens cap still on the telescope, a shadow effect does admittedly occur. However, it is not the shadow of God; it is the shadow of the plastic lens cap, *espáz.*

OR

Somewhere in those Dickinsonian ellipses after "beauty" lies a phrase like "...which is when something bad happens to someone I hate, like my ex-wife Timber, etc. etc." The fact that, as far as we know, Mistral was neither a lesbian nor married to my ex-wife is irrelevant. Everybody hates somebody, and there's nothing more beautiful than *laughing at your enemy's misfortune.*

The correct answer? Both. And though I can't prove the second part (Borges writes eloquently of the first in a Valentine letter to another Borges, living precisely three seconds behind the normal Borges), we can be certain I'm on the right track. And Timber, don't think you're above suspicion. You are a shameless social climber, and I wouldn't be surprised if, in addition to tramping around the bar at the St. Regis with your paid *claquers,* you didn't try to make a pass at Mistral even though you were just an itch on your Dad's crotch when she died.

HELEN KELLER: *"The most beautiful things in the world cannot be seen or even touched, they must be felt with the heart."*

Please. I don't know where to start, so I'll just finish: The most beautiful things *can* be touched. You just have to pay to do it. (See above: The Bottoms Up Lounge).

ALBERT EINSTEIN: *"The most beautiful thing we can experience is the mysterious."*

Einstein gets credibility in all aesthetic domains because of his beautiful mind and – usually – spot-on observations about the theoretical and natural world. That's giving this horse a lot of head, despite the need to put the huge hair part of the eminent physicist's head in whatever that expression means.

The mysterious is lots of things, but it's usually not beautiful – it's usually a flaming bag of ordure on my doorstep, the way a woman blows a rape whistle when I'm just trying to get directions to NYU for a lecture on Kant; or how my roommate Clint's rent check manages to take a tenor of eternal death, yet his hydroponically grown marijuana crop in our closet remains fecund as can be. No, the most beautiful thing we can experience is not "the mysterious." If Einstein could go back in time – which he may actually be doing – and utter one more profound glottal stop and suck his tongue in contemplation, I think he'd have to agree that the most beautiful thing we can experience is the obvious: *Regularly occurring and marginally deviant sex atop piles of money* (tax-free). Maybe in the Caribbean or somewhere – a little drunk, but not too.

"Hey! This is all subjective," you may snort, ruining the moment and sounding a lot like Aristotle, who didn't have a postgraduate degree and dressed like a prick. Beauty, like love, is not *one* thing. It is, like love and STDs, a many-splendored thing: an octopus with each tentacle representing an independent yet critical tributary sluicing through eternity and the divine and water, no one arm more important than the other, but all necessary unless you want to try dealing with a septopus (not beautiful and also petulant). I hope this treatise clears up a few misbegotten notions about what beauty is, precisely:

It's my *new* girlfriend, Timber! Take *that*.

And the next time you feel like posting on Facebook that the ex-wife looks like four albino radii intersecting in a Quiche Lorraine, maybe you'll take to heart the words of Clint, who argues, "Timber's nothing but trouble, dude. It's fine, though, how she can cover her pussy hair with her head hair."

Clint, too? It's all just so *ugly*.

IMAGE CREDITS

CONTRIBUTORS

ROBIN ANTALEK is the author of *The Summer We Fell Apart* (HarperCollins, 2010), chosen as a Target Breakout Book and soon to be published in Turkey by Artemis Yayinlari. She lives in Saratoga Springs, NY, with her husband and children. You can visit her Web site at robinantalek.com, or if brave enough, publicly admit to liking her on Facebook.

MATTHEW BALDWIN is a writer, raconteur, and all-around gentleman rogue from San Diego, California. He earned a B.A. from the University of California in 2001 and an MFA from the University of New Orleans in 2004. A regular nonfiction contributor to *The Nervous Breakdown*, he has also published fiction and poetry in several smaller literary journals and online literary sites. In his spare time he is a professional martial arts instructor. Baldwin is currently at work on both a novel and a collection of postcard-sized flash fiction.

JESSICA ANYA BLAU'S newest novel, *Drinking Closer to Home* (HarperCollins/Harper Perennial), has been called "a raging success" and "unrelentingly side-splittingly funny." It was featured in Target stores as a "Breakout Book" and made many Best Books of the Year lists for 2011. Her first novel, *The Summer of Naked Swim Parties* (HarperCollins/Harper Perennial), was picked as a Best Summer Book by *The Today Show*, *The New York Post*, and *New York Magazine*. *The San Francisco Chronicle* and other newspapers chose it as one of the best books of the year. Jessica's third novel, *The Wonder Bread Summer* (HarperCollins/Harper Perennial) is coming out in the summer of 2013. Jessica wrote the screenplay for *Franny*, a film starring Frances Fisher and Steve Howey. *Franny* is now in post-production in Los Angeles. Currently Jessica is a Visiting Assistant Professor at Goucher College. She also teaches at Johns Hopkins University where she attended The Writing Seminars.

NORA BURKEY recently completed her B.A. in creative writing from Eugene Lang College, The New School for Liberal Arts in New York City. She has been published in *The Furnace Review*, an online literary magazine for fiction and poetry. She currently lives in Toronto, Ontario, but hails from the suburbs of Philadelphia.

ELIZABETH COLLINS has had essays, stories, and articles published in *Columbia: A Journal of Literature and Art*; *Natural Bridge*; *The Massachusetts Review*; *Bookslut*; and in various newspapers and magazines. She is a journalist and college writing instructor, and a tutor, artist, and blogger (prettyfreaky.blogspot.com). Collins is also a graduate of the University of Iowa's MFA program in English/Writing, and she won the Columbia University Nonfiction Prize. Collins' memoir, *Too Cool for School*, will be published in early 2012, with her young adult novels to follow. She lives with her family near Philadelphia. Follow her on Twitter @sheepandstars.

RONLYN DOMINGUE is the author of *The Mercy of Thin Air* (Atria Books, 2005). This debut novel was a 2005 Borders Original Voices Award Finalist and was acquired in eleven other countries. Her second and third novels are forthcoming from Atria Books, scheduled for Spring 2013 and Spring 2014. Her writing has appeared in *New England Review*; *Clackamas Literary Review*; *New Delta Review*; *The*

Independent (UK); and *Shambhala Sun*. In the past, Ronlyn worked as a grassroots organizer, project manager, teacher, and grant writer. Visit her at ronlyndomingue.com.

MELISSA FEBOS is the author of *Whip Smart* (2010), a critically acclaimed memoir of her work as a professional dominatrix while she was studying at The New School. Febos has also contributed to *The New York Times*; *Hunger Mountain*; *Dissent*; *The Southeast Review*; *Redivider*; *The Rambler*; *The Huffington Post*; *Bitch Magazine*; and *The Chronicle of Higher Education*. She is an assistant professor of English at Utica College.

RICH FERGUSON has performed across the country and has been heard on many radio stations. He has shared the same stage with Patti Smith and Janet Hamill, Exene Cervenka, David Thomas of Pere Ubu, Holly Prado, and many other esteemed poets and musicians. He has performed at the Redcat Theater in Disney Hall, the Electric Lodge (Venice, CA), The Knitting Factory (NYC & LA), the South by Southwest Music Festival, the North by Northwest Music Festival, the Henry Miller Library, Tongue and Groove, Beyond Baroque, and the Topanga Film Festival. On the college circuit he has performed at UC Irvine, UC-Santa Barbara, UCLA, El Camino College, and Cal State Northridge. He is a featured performer in the sequel to the film *1 Giant Leap*. It's called *What About Me*, and also features Michael Stipe, Michael Franti, k.d. lang, Krishna Das, and others. Ferguson has studied poetry with Allen Ginsberg and fiction writing with Aimee Bender and Sid Stebel. In addition, he has been published in the *Los Angeles Times*, spotlighted on PBS (*Egg: The Art Show*), is a regular contributor to *The Nervous*

Breakdown, and his spoken word/music CD, entitled *Where I Come From,* was produced by Herb Graham Jr. (John Cale, Macy Gray).

M.J. FIEVRE, born in Port-au-Prince, is an expatriate whose short stories and poems have appeared in numerous publications, including *Haiti Noir* (Akashic Books, 2010); *The Southeast Review*; *The Caribbean Writer*; and *The Mom Egg.* She is currently a graduate student in the creative writing program at Florida International University. She loves coconut shrimp, piña coladas, her dog Wiskee, and a good story. Anton Chekhov is one of her favorite writers. Her author Web site is located at lominy.com.

J.E. FISHMAN is making plans while God laughs. He is at work with actor Tom Teti on a screenplay entitled "The Wisest Wiseguy," about two retired mafia dons who attempt to resolve a nature-nurture debate with a reality contest. His mystery novel, *Cadaver Blues,* was serialized this year on *The Nervous Breakdown*, and his thriller, *Primacy* (Verbitrage, 2011), just hit stores. Follow his adventures in new book publishing on Tumblr at *A Third Way*, and his thoughts on writing and publishing on his personal blog. You can also read about his long-suffering tennis game at *An Ungrateful Game* and follow him on Twitter @jefishman.

GINA FRANGELLO is the fiction editor of *The Nervous Breakdown.* She is the author of the collection *Slut Lullabies* (Emergency Press, 2010) and the novel *My Sister's Continent.* She was the longtime editor of the literary magazine *Other Voices* and co-founded its book imprint, *Other Voices Books*, where she is now the executive editor of the Chicago office. Her short stories have been published in many lit mags and anthologies, including *A Stranger Among Us: Stories of Cross Cultural Collision and Connection*; *Prairie Schooner*; *StoryQuarterly*; *Swink*; and *Clackamas Literary Review*. She guest edited the anthology *Falling Backwards: Stories of Fathers and Daughters* and teaches creative writing at Columbia College Chicago and Northwestern University's School of Continuing Studies. Gina lives in Chicago and can be found online at Facebook, or on her Web site, ginafrangello.com. She has twin daughters, a wild preschooler son, and never sleeps.

MARNI GROSSMAN holds a B.A. from Vassar in Women's Studies. The degree turned out to be of little practical value, but nonetheless holds a lot of sentimental weight. She's written for *BUST*; *Playgirl*; *Heeb*; *Sadie* magazine; and *gURL.com*. You can also find her work in the anthology *Click: When We Knew We Were Feminists* (Seal Press, 2010). Her interests include subverting the patriarchy, reading, and *Law and Order*, the Jerry Orbach years. She is currently studying for her masters in social work at New York University.

JAMES D. IRWIN is a British writer and occasional comedian. As well as his nonfiction writing at *The Nervous Breakdown* and various other small publications, Irwin has written an unpublished novel with a twist ending of M. Night Shyamalan proportions and directed a short film with the production quality and erotic value of Paris Hilton's sex tape. He currently runs The Late Train Comedy Night in Winchester and is preparing to direct his first play at a local festival. As a true Englishman, his only interests besides writing are tea, cricket, and aesthetically displeasing dentistry.

QUENBY MOONE, nonfiction editor at *The Nervous Breakdown*, used to be a graphic designer who wrote once in a while. After her father came down with a touch of Stage IV prostate cancer, she became a writer who did graphic design once in a while. She's written a book called *Living in Twilight* (no relation to vampires, unless dying of cancer is a part of Edward's story), which meshes her graphic design skills with her words.

UCHE OGBUJI was born in Calabar, Nigeria. He lived, among other places, in Egypt and England before settling near Boulder, Colorado where he lives with his wife and four children. Uche is a computer engineer (trained in Nigeria and the USA) and entrepreneur whose abiding passion is poetry. His poems, fusing his native Igbo culture, European Classicism, Western American setting, and Hip-Hop style, have appeared or are forthcoming in journals and anthologies including *ELF: Eclectic Literary Forum*; *Corium Magazine*; *Soundzine*; *Lucid Rhythms*; *The Flea*; *IthacaLit*; *Unsplendid*; *String Poet*; *Mountain Gazette*; *The Raintown Review*; *Verse Wisconsin* and *New Sun Rising: Stories for Japan*. He is poetry editor and essayist at *The Nervous Breakdown*. Uche also snowboards, coaches and plays soccer, and trains in American Kenpo. Visit him at uche.ogbuji.net or keep up with him on twitter (@uogbuji).

GREG OLEAR, the senior editor of *The Nervous Breakdown*, teaches creative writing at Manhattanville College. His work has appeared at *The Rumpus*; *Babble.com*; *The Millions*; *Chronogram*; *WhAP!*; and *Hudson Valley Magazine*. His 2009 debut novel, *Totally Killer* (Harper, 2009), was featured at the Quais du Polar noir festival in Lyon, France, where he was a panelist. *Fathermucker* (Harper, 2011) is his acclaimed second novel. He lives with his wife, Stephanie St. John, and two children in New Paltz, NY.

VICTORIA PATTERSON is the author of the novel *This Vacant Paradise* (Counterpoint Press, 2011). *Drift* (Mariner Books, 2009), her collection of interlinked short stories, was a finalist for the California Book Award and the 2009 Story Prize. *The San Francisco Chronicle* selected *Drift* as one of the best books of 2009. Her work has appeared in various publications and journals, including the *Los Angeles Times*; *Alaska Quarterly Review*; and *The Southern Review*. She lives with her family in Southern California and is an instructor at Antioch University's Master of Fine Arts program.

RACHEL POLLON lives, loves, and writes in Los Angeles, CA. Some of her experiences include being employed in both the music and television industries, committing to lies when she's done something embarrassing and needs to cover it up, deciding what to have for dinner, and being a loyal friend, family member, sexual partner, and dog owner. Her aim is to write about the interesting bits. And to see her neuroses as gifts she might like to return, but instead puts in a closet and forgets about until she goes looking for her favorite pair of boots and is slapped in the face by shame and recognition. She is a contributor to *The Nervous Breakdown*, and her blog is at seismicdrift.com.

JUDY PRINCE, a retired college teacher and union activist, now lives half the year in Norfolk, Virginia, and the other half in Darlington, UK. She has published articles in the *Los Angeles Times* and the *Virginian-Pilot* and was a Chicago Dramatists Short Plays Competition finalist. She is now at work on a play about Shakespeare the woman, and recently launched Frisky Moll Press with the poetry pamphlets of Robin Hamilton (Anacreon translations) and Patrick McManus (*On the Dig*). Her own poetry pamphlets have been published by Phantom Rooster Press (2006 and 2009). Prince's work is included in the first *James Kirkup Memorial Poetry Competition Anthology* (Red Squirrel Press, UK, 2010). Her *Poems2* is reviewed in *SPHINX 12* (HappenStance Press).

LANCE REYNALD was born in Texas, raised in Washington, DC, and self-exiled to Colorado. This world-traveled collector of air miles currently lives in Portland, Oregon, but keeps a bag packed near the door for the moment when wanderlust calls. He has an affinity for vanilla lattes, dirty martinis, the works of Faulkner, Kerouac, and Burroughs, the smell of imported cigarettes in fine woolens, the photography of Doisneau and Brassai, and what some regard as the worst of early 1980s Brit Pop. His first novel, *Pop Salvation* (Harper Perennial, 2009), is now available wherever books are sold.

STEPHANIE ST. JOHN is a singer-songwriter who has recorded five full-length albums: the solo LP *Cinderella's Dead*; *Vee Khan Nez Pha* and *Cease to Thrill*, with Vdisc; Lazy Eyes' *Tokyo Could Not Be Opened Because Tokyo Could Not Be Found*, with avant-garde composer David First; and *250 Times Sweeter Than Sugar*, with her band, Mimi Ferocious. She has performed at the Whisky A Go Go and The Roxy (in Los Angeles), CBGB and Brownies (in New York), and the general assembly room at the UN (in every country at once). Her latest projects include *The Blanket Show*, an album of experimental children's music she's producing with First, and a new as-yet-untitled solo record. She lives with her husband (Greg Olear) and two children in New Paltz, NY.

STEVE SPARSHOTT, a British citizen and formerly a professional model maker, turned to writing after brain damage sustained in a 2003 road accident caused him to lose much of his physical function. Typing with the three middle fingers of his left hand at a blistering fifteen words per minute, he has had work printed in the London literary magazine *Smoke*, and various academic publications have featured his design-related social criticism. He reviews films for *Screenjabber.com* and, because his life just isn't difficult enough, he's writing a memoir called *Get Well Soon*.

TYLER STODDARD SMITH, described as an "up-and-coming humorist" by *Esquire* magazine, has had his works featured in *The McSweeney's Joke Book of Book Jokes*; *The Best American Fantasy*; *Esquire*; *Meridian*; *Pindeldyboz*; *The Big Jewel*; *Yankee Pot Roast*; *Word Riot*; *Barrelhouse*; *Monkeybicycle*; and *McSweeney's*, among others. Visit his website at tylerstoddardsmith.wordpress.com.

CATHERINE TUFARIELLO's first book of poems, *Keeping My Name* (Texas Tech UP), was a finalist for the 2005 *Los Angeles Times* Book Prize in Poetry and the winner of the 2006 Poets' Prize. Her poems have been featured in *The Writers' Almanac*; *American Life in Poetry*; and *Poetry Daily*; and have been anthologized in *The Seagull Reader*; *Western Wind*; *The Sparrow Book of New American Poets*; and elsewhere. A native of Buffalo, NY, Catherine lives with her husband and daughter in Valparaiso, Indiana, where she works at Valparaiso University's Center for Civic Reflection.

ANGELA TUNG has had fiction and nonfiction published in *The Frisky*; *Matador Life*; *The New York Press*; and *Carve Magazine*. She earned an M.A. in creative writing from Boston University and can be found at angelatung.com. Tung's young adult novel, *Song of the Stranger*, was published by Roxbury Park Books (1999). Her latest book, *Black Fish: Memoir of a Bad Luck Girl*, chronicles the failed marriage between a Chinese woman and Korean man, both American-born but still bound by old-world traditions and is available on Amazon. Tung lives in San Francisco.

STEPHEN WALTER is an independent bookseller in Princeton, New Jersey. He feels it would be awkward to say more.

ZOE ZOLBROD has written one novel, *Currency* (OV Books, 2010), but she worked on it for a very long time. She's written some short stories, too, and a few of them were published here and there way back when. Also, she's written essays, some of which appeared in *Maxine*, a 'zine she co-published in the 1990s. She was born in Meadville, Pennsylvania, went to college in Oberlin, Ohio, and got an M.A. from the University of Illinois at Chicago. She works in educational publishing and lives in Evanston, IL, with her husband, the artist Mark DeBernardi, and their son and daughter.

ACKNOWLEDGMENTS

Tremendous thanks must be given to all the writers and artists who so willingly shared their work for this anthology. Thank you also to our intrepid interns, Jen Schiller, Alex Meyer, and Shiah Irgangladen, all of whom worked with blazing speed and impressive skill. Sincere thanks go to designer Charlotte Howard who worked tirelessly (but with great humor) on this book, to Evre Başak for her wonderful cover artwork, and to proofreader Chris Gage. A million thanks go to Brad Listi, founder of *The Nervous Breakdown* and publisher of TNB Books, as well as every writer/editor and reader who makes *The Nervous Breakdown* such a welcoming online home and a fount of literary innovation.

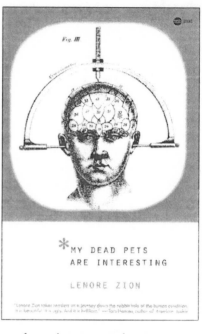

Subversia
by D.R. Haney

"Haney interweaves tiny details with weighty subjects deftly, through articles smartly ordered for just the right balance of thematic lilt and interest-holding lurch."
—Matt Cook, *Pank Magazine*

In this bare-knuckled, frankly autobiographical collection, D.R. Haney shares essays on his struggles and artistic evolution; from punk rock malcontent in 1980s New York, to B-movie actor in Roger Corman films; to screenwriter on *Friday the 13th: Part VII*; to expatriate writer in Serbia; to author of the celebrated underground novel *Banned for Life*. *Subversia* is written with the bracing candor and lyrical beauty that have earned Haney a cult following worldwide. (240 pp)

Paper Doll Orgy
Drawings by Ted McCagg

"Ted McCagg is a truly original thinker who really makes me laugh. And for that, I hate him."
—Conan O'Brien

For the first time, Ted McCagg's cartoons are collected where they have always longed to live: the printed page. His work, which has won him a legion of fans throughout cyberspace, is a regular feature on *The Nervous Breakdown*, and has appeared elsewhere on the web at *The Atlantic*, *The Washington Post*, and *Laughing Squid*. (208 pp)

CPSIA information can be obtained at www.ICGtesting.com
Printed in the USA
BVOW07s0825141113

336218BV00002B/39/P